D1265562

The Mailbox® 2015–2016 Preschool Yearbook

372.21
MAI
2015-2016
70-8670

Managing Editor, *The Mailbox* Magazine: Kimberly A. Brugger

Editorial Team: Becky S. Andrews, Diane Badden, Kimberley Bruck, Karen A. Brudnak, Pam Crane, Chris Curry, Karen Brewer Grossman, Tazmen Fisher Hansen, Marsha Heim, Lori Z. Henry, Troy Lawrence, Kitty Lowrance, Rachel Morales, Tina Petersen, Gary Phillips (COVER ARTIST), Mark Rainey, Rebecca Saunders, Sharon M. Tresino

ISBN 978-1-61276-643-0
ISSN 1088-5536

©2016 The Education Center, LLC, PO Box 9753, Greensboro, NC 27429-0753

Printed in the United States of America.

The Mailbox® Yearbook
PO Box 6189
Harlan, IA 51593-1689

Look for *The Mailbox*® *2016–2017 Preschool Yearbook* in the summer of 2017. The Education Center, LLC, is the publisher of *The Mailbox*®, *Teacher's Helper*®, and *Learning*® magazines, as well as other fine products. Call 866.477.4273 or visit TheMailbox.com.

Contents

Departments

Features

Literacy Units

Math Units

Teacher Resource Units

Thematic Units

Index

TheMailbox.com

Arts & Crafts for Little Hands

Arts & Crafts
for Little Hands

Crayon Characters

In advance, make large crayon cutouts in several different colors and collect colorful craft items. Cut black strips of construction paper for arms and legs. To begin, choose a crayon. Next, glue to your crayon craft items of the same color. Draw a face. Then accordion-fold the arms and legs and attach them to complete the project.

Christina Sioss and Stephanie Seto
Public School 105
Brooklyn, NY

Process Art

We Love Fall!

To make these simple and adorable projects, gather several heart-shaped sponges and place each one near a different container of fall-colored paint. Choose a sponge and press it in the paint. Then make prints on the paper. Continue in the same way to make several colorful heart prints. When the paint is dry, draw veins on the hearts to transform them into leaves. How lovely!

Deborah J. Ryan
Newberg, OR

Drizzle and Press

Here's a colorful process-art masterpiece! Gather a paper plate, plastic spoons, tissue paper scraps, and containers of tinted glue. Drizzle the colorful glue on the plate. Then crumple the tissue paper and press it on the glue. Gorgeous!

 tip To make this a seasonal project, use glue and tissue paper in colors that relate to the current holiday or season!

Process Art

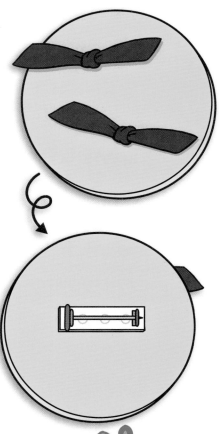

Nighttime Flyby

These cute little accessories make adorable Halloween gifts! Paint a three-inch wood circle yellow so it resembles a moon. (Wood circles are available at craft stores.) Cut two short lengths of black ribbon and tie a knot in the middle of each one (bat). Then glue the bats to the moon. Hot-glue (for teacher use only) a pin to the back of the moon.

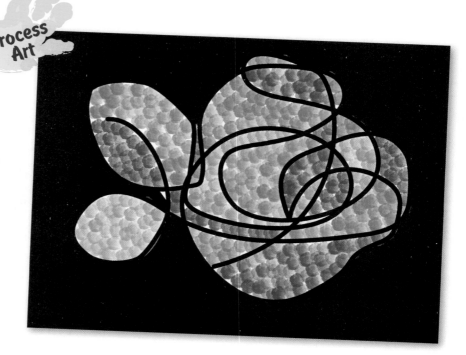

Squiggle Art

This lovely artwork looks fabulous displayed in a hallway! Use a marker to draw a scribble on a sheet of paper. Then use bingo daubers to fill in some of the spaces. Finally, cut out the design (with help as needed) and glue the resulting artwork to a sheet of black paper. Gorgeous!

Pumpkin-Top Prints!

After a pumpkin-carving experience, use the top of your resulting jack-o'-lantern for some fabulous artwork! Place the top on a table along with paint and a paintbrush. Hold the top by the stem and then paint the underside. Next, press it on a sheet of paper and then remove it. Repeat the process until you're happy with your artwork.

Arts-and-Crafts Special

Pom-Poms + Cardboard Tubes = Art!

Do you have pom-poms and cardboard tubes? Have your little ones make some fabulous process art!

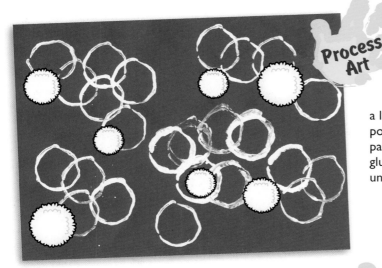

Process Art

Cloudy Sky

Get a small cardboard tube (or cut a piece from a large tube), a shallow pan of white paint, white pom-poms, and glue. Press the cardboard tube in the paint and make prints on a blue sheet of paper. Next, glue white pom-poms to the paper. The result is a unique cloudy sky!

Process Art

Tap and Roll

Here's a terrific way to explore texture. Glue a pom-pom to a craft stick and wrap rubber bands around a large cardboard tube. Use a foam roller to roll different colors of paint on a sheet of paper. To add texture, roll or drag the cardboard tube on the paint. Then hold the craft stick and tap the pom-pom on the paint. Lovely!

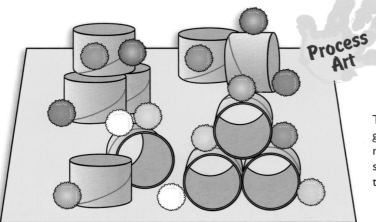

Process Art

Sassy Sculpture!

This free-form artwork helps to build spatial skills. To make one, cut cardboard tubes into thin rings and get colorful pom-poms and glue. Use glue to attach rings and pom-poms to a sheet of tagboard to create a sculpture, being sure to experiment with different ways the items can be arranged.

Arts & Crafts
for Little Hands

Balloon-Print Leaves

To prepare for this colorful fall artwork, place three puddles of fall-colored paint in one tray and blow up a balloon. Dip the balloon quickly into the paint and then pat it on a sheet of paper. Repeat the process several times. After the paint has dried, cut a leaf shape from the paper. Lovely!

Mindi Morton
Mindi's Oak Tree Preschool
North San Juan, CA

Process Art

Process Art

Textured Tape

To make a design, a youngster tears various lengths of masking tape and arranges them on a sheet of paper as desired, overlapping the tape pieces to create dimension. Then he uses clear tape to lightly tape another sheet of paper on top of the design. He rubs the sides of different-colored crayons over the paper until the design is revealed.

Golden Gelt

This process art is perfect for Hanukkah! Gather small cylindrical containers, a shallow pan of paint, gold sequins, and gold glitter. Dip a container in the paint and make prints on a sheet of paper. Then sprinkle sequins and glitter over the wet paint. What lovely, glittery gelt!

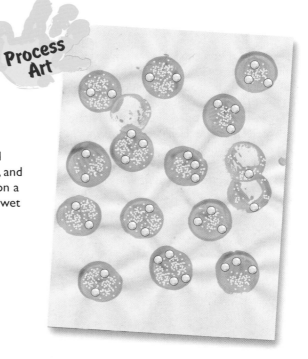

Process Art

Quick and Easy Wreath

This zippy little craft is fun and easy. To make one, cut the middle from an uncoated paper plate. (Recycle the middle or save it for another craft.) Then color the plate rim green. Next, use a red bingo dauber to make dots on the green so they look like holly berries. Use thick ribbon to make a bow and attach it to the wreath.

Janet Boyce
Hinojosa Early Childhood and Pre-Kindergarten Center
Houston, TX

Sweet Little Angel

This craft can be either a shelf decoration or a tree ornament! Make a cutout similar to the one shown. Then use a hole puncher to make holes along the bottom of the cutout. Draw a face where indicated and then roll the cutout and tape it in place to make the angel's body. Next, gather a coffee filter in the middle and secure it in place with a piece of pipe cleaner so it resembles wings. Also form a second piece of pipe cleaner to make a halo. Then use a hot-glue gun to attach the wings and halo. (Hot glue is for teacher use only.) Attach a hanger to the craft if using it as a tree ornament.

Deborah J. Ryan
Newberg, OR

Process Art

Fantastic Foil

For this process art project, gather heavy-duty aluminum foil, a sheet of tagboard, and shallow containers of colorful tempera paint. To begin, crumple and mold aluminum foil sheets to create irregular-shaped stampers. Then dip a stamper in paint and press it on the tagboard. Repeat the process with other foil stampers and colors of paint.

tip → To frame your artwork, crumple, mold, or twist aluminum foil and glue it to the edges of the tagboard.

What Can You Do With Pinecones?

You find them all over the ground around this time of year. But what can you do with them? We have a few ideas!

Turkey Time

To make these pinecone turkeys, write your name on a sheet of waxed paper. Then lay a pinecone down on the paper. Drizzle glue over the back of the pinecone. Then insert feathers into the glue. Next, cut out a simple turkey head similar to the shape shown. Then glue a beak and wattle to the head. Drizzle glue on the bottom of the cutout and slide it into the pinecone. What a cute turkey!

Linda Heavrin
Benton, IL

Glue It On!

This process art activity is perfect for an art center! To make one, get a large pinecone and a variety of craft materials, such as small pom-poms, sequins, glitter, pieces of yarn and ribbon, and scraps of tissue paper. Glue materials to the pinecone as desired.

Process Art

Pinecone Press

Gather large pinecones with reasonably flat bottoms and place them near shallow containers of paint. Choose a pinecone, press it into the paint, and then press it onto a sheet of paper. Repeat the process with other pinecones and colors of paint until you're satisfied with your masterpiece!

Baking Cup Snowflake

Who knew little muffin cup liners could make such a decorative snowflake!

Supplies:

12 mini paper baking cups	paintbrush
12" length of yarn	3 craft sticks
hot glue gun (for teacher use)	glitter
white tempera paint	glue

Setup:

Hot-glue the craft sticks to make a snowflake shape. Tie the yarn into a loop.

Steps:

1. Paint both sides of the snowflake white.
2. Sprinkle glitter on the wet paint. Allow the paint to dry.
3. Glue six baking cups to one side of the snowflake and then allow the glue to dry.
4. Glue six more baking cups to the other side of the snowflake. Before adding the last liner, sandwich the yarn loop between the snowflake and liner to make a hanger. Allow the glue to dry.

Recycled Snowman

To make this snowman cutie, gather two short cardboard tubes. Then cut a small section from one tube so that you have one whole tube plus two tube pieces, all in different lengths. Staple the tubes in a stack as shown. Then staple the stack to a large index card or piece of tagboard. Paint the stack of tubes white. Then use paint or paper to add features and buttons to the snowman. Stuff cotton batting into the tubes and arrange a strip of fabric so it resembles a scarf. Then glue it in place.

Mary Ann Craven
Fallbrook United Methodist School
Fallbrook, CA

Want to add a hat? Simply roll a 1½" x 4" piece of black construction paper into a tube and secure it with staples. Then attach the tube to a 2½-inch black construction paper circle. Attach the resulting top hat to the snowman.

Process Art

"Heart-y" Art!

This lovely process art looks great displayed for Valentine's Day! Place a heart cookie cutter next to a shallow pan of red paint. Place an unused toothbrush next to a shallow pan of pink paint. Then dip the cookie cutter in the red paint and make prints on a sheet of white paper. Next, dip the toothbrush in the pink paint. Then tap the brush on the index finger of your opposite hand to add pink splatters to the paper. For an extra fun touch, finish off the artwork with heart stickers.

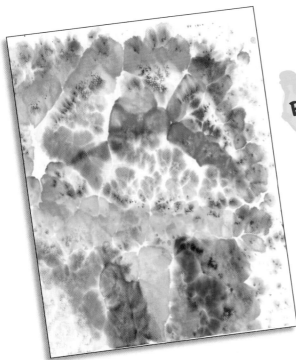

Process Art

Terrific Tie-Dye

This masterpiece is covered with gorgeous color! To make one, color a sheet of white paper towel with washable markers. Then place the towel on top of a sheet of white construction paper. Use a spray bottle of water to generously spray the paper towel. Then lift and discard the paper towel.

Noodle Soup Art

Process Art

Little ones will love this pasta process art! To make the project, glue different types of pasta to a sheet of construction paper. When the glue is dry, paint the pasta and the paper a variety of colors. Now that looks tasty!

Deborah J. Ryan
Newberg, OR

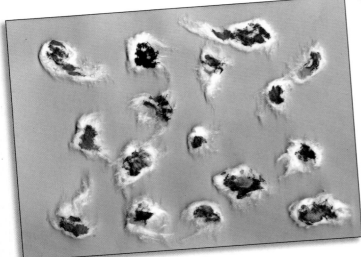

Process Art

Colorful Cotton Balls

Can you use watercolors to paint cotton balls? Well, why not? Pull apart several cotton balls. Next, drop white glue on a sheet of colorful construction paper. Then press pieces of cotton balls on the glue. Load a paintbrush with water and a desired paint color. Then touch it to the cotton to transfer the color. Continue until you're satisfied with the results.

Janet Boyce
Hinojosa Early Childhood and Pre-Kindergarten Center
Houston, TX

Soaking Up Art: Projects with Sponges!

Process Art

Check out these engaging art projects that use sponges in different ways.

ideas contributed by Janet Boyce
Hinojosa Early Childhood and Pre-Kindergarten Center
Houston, TX

Pretty Prints

Get an extra large sponge and dampen it. Then use tempera paints to paint the sponge. Next, press the painted side of the sponge on a sheet of paper several times. If desired, repaint the sponge and repeat the activity.

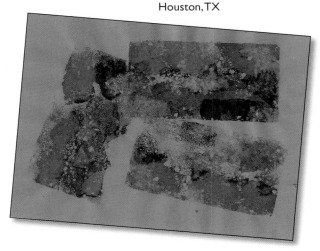

Fold and Paint

Fold a sheet of construction paper in half and then unfold it. Next, dip pieces of a sponge in paint and then arrange them on one half of the paper. Refold the paper and then smooth it over with your hand, pressing down. Open the paper, remove the sponge pieces, and reveal your artwork!

Soak It Up!

Paint with watercolors on a sheet of paper, making sure to use a lot of water. Then take a dry (or mostly dry) piece of sponge and press it on your painting for several seconds. Remove the sponge and notice that it soaked up some of the paint. Continue, removing paint as desired, until you're satisfied with your artwork.

Handprint Pot of Gold!

To make this handprint craft, paint your palm black. Then paint colorful stripes on the fingers, omitting the thumb. Press your hand on a sheet of construction paper. The print will resemble a pot with a rainbow! Then drizzle glue between the pot and the rainbow and sprinkle gold glitter on the glue.

Lindsey Ellingwood
Slaughter Road Child Development Center
Madison, AL

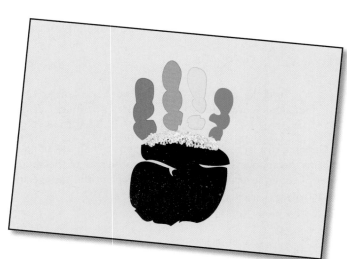

/u/, /u/, Up!

Build phonological awareness skills with this activity. Prepare a variety of one-inch-wide construction paper strips. To begin, cut a piece off a strip. Then snip two corners so the piece resembles an arrow. Glue the arrow to a sheet of colorful paper so it's pointing upward. Then say, "/u/, /u/, up!" Continue until the paper is filled with colorful arrows!

Janet Boyce
Hinojosa Early Childhood and Pre-Kindergarten Center
Houston, TX

Process Art

Shiny Showers

To make this simple and lovely process art, tear strips of aluminum foil and glue the strips to a sheet of blue construction paper as desired. Then brush diluted glue on the foil and press torn strips of white or gray tissue paper to the page. If needed, brush another layer of diluted glue on the tissue paper.

Deborah J. Ryan
Newberg, OR

Pasta Bird Nests

Get bird's nest pasta from your local grocery store. Then paint a pasta nest brown. Next, glue a paper beak and mini wiggle eyes to a large blue pom-pom (bluebird). Glue the bluebird to the nest.

Jaclyn Hicks
Ducklings Early Learning Center
Kennett Square, PA

To display the nest projects, glue them to a branch and then hang the branch in your classroom or display the branch on a shelf!

Arts & Crafts
for Little Hands

A Flowery Card

This sweet project makes a terrific Mother's Day Gift! To make one, fold a 5" x 6" rectangular piece of paper to make a cone and flatten it as shown. Glue or tape it in place as needed. Attach the flattened cone to a construction paper card. Next, slide green construction paper strips (stems) into the cone and glue them in place. Then crumple squares of tissue paper and glue them to the tops of the stems. Write the message shown and your name in the card.

Lourdes Geiger
Claywell Elementary
Tampa, FL

Mom.
I love you
a bunch!

Ethan

Create a Clown

Here's a fun craft that's perfect following a circus field trip or theme! Use watercolors to paint a paper circle. When the paint is dry, attach eye, nose, and mouth cutouts as shown. Then glue paper shreds or accordion-folded strips for hair. Hilarious!

Audrey Glover
Soapstone Preschool
Raleigh, NC

Shiny Yellow Sun

Spotlight sunny weather with this brilliant craft!

Materials for one:

white fingerpaint paper
small white paper plate
fork
yellow paint

paintbrush
gold glitter
glue

Setup:

Trace the paper plate onto the center of the paper.

Steps:

1. Paint the back of the plate; then sprinkle glitter on the wet paint.
2. Fingerpaint the paper around the outside of the circle.
3. To make the sun's rays, drag the fork's tines through the wet paint from the tracing toward each edge of the paper.
4. Glue the paper plate on the circle.

Process Art

It's a Home Run!

This twist on marble painting is perfect for sports fans! To make this project, place a sheet of paper in a lidded plastic container. Then dip a baseball in several colors of paint. Place the baseball on the paper and securely fasten the lid. Then shake and tilt the container as desired. When finished, remove the lid to reveal your artwork!

Janet Diltz
Delwood Preschool
Delmar, IA

Fabulous Foil Paintings

These unique and shiny paintings look stunning displayed in a hallway or classroom!

Supplies:
8" x 10" piece of heavy-duty foil
tempera paint
paintbrush
2 sheets of 9" x 12" construction paper
scissors
glue

Steps:
1. Paint individual objects or designs on the foil. Allow time for the paint to dry.
2. Glue the foil to a sheet of construction paper. Let the glue dry.
3. Cut around your designs.
4. Glue them to the other sheet of paper.

Process Art

Process Art

Geometric Designs

For this engaging process art, cut a supply of four-inch squares from magazine pages. Then fold a square in half to form a rectangle or a triangle and glue the folded halves together. Next, glue the shape to a sheet of construction paper. Continue with other squares as desired.

BUSY KIDS®

Busy Kids®

Fine- and Gross-Motor Activities for Developing Little Muscles and Big Muscles

Fine motor

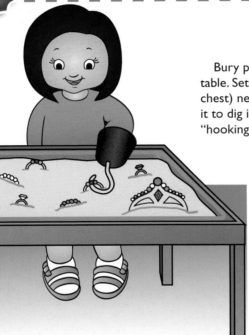

Hooked!

Bury plastic tiaras, necklaces, bracelets, and rings in a sand table. Set a pair of plastic pirate hooks and a tub (treasure chest) nearby. A child places a hook on a hand and uses it to dig in the sand and search for buried treasure. After "hooking" treasure, she places it in the treasure chest.

Janet Boyce
Hinojosa Early Childhood and Pre-Kindergarten Center
Houston, TX

tip → An Internet shopping search will turn up plenty of inexpensive options for pirate hooks!

Gross motor

Make a Snake

Set a tub of linking cubes on the floor and place a cube near it. This cube will be the beginning of a snake. Direct little ones to line up a few feet away from the cubes. As you time youngsters, have them take turns running to the tub, attaching one cube to the snake, and then going to the back of the line. Continue until all youngsters have added a cube. Invite students to repeat the activity a few times, encouraging them to beat their best time each round. Depending on the skill of your youngsters, you could divide the class into two teams and complete the activity as a relay!

Margaret Aumen, Emory United Methodist Nursery School
New Oxford, PA

Spray and Count

Program an inexpensive shower curtain liner with numbers. Attach the liner to a fence or other structure in your outdoor play area and place squirt bottles filled with water nearby. Name a number and have the child spray that number a matching number of times.

Margaret Aumen
Emory United Methodist Nursery
    School
New Oxford, PA

1   3   5
8   2   6
9   4   7

Watch Out for Kitty!

Arrange several plastic hoops (mouse holes) in a large open area. Invite a couple of youngsters to be the cats. Have the cats lay on the floor near the mouse holes and pretend to be sleeping. Direct the remaining students (mice) to stand in the mouse holes. As you sing the first verse of the song shown, have the mice run around the area. As you sing the second verse of the song, direct each cat to get up and try to tag a mouse before it returns to its mouse hole. The tagged mice are the cats during the next round of the game.

(sung to the tune of "The Farmer in the Dell")

The kitties are asleep.
The kitties are asleep.
Heigh-ho, the derry-o,
The kitties are asleep.

The kitties are awake.
The kitties are awake.
Heigh-ho, the derry-o,
The kitties are awake.

Diane Colon, Pettisville Christian Preschool, Pettisville, OH

Coconut Dough

Add coconut flavoring to a batch of white play dough. Place the play dough and a coconut at a table. A child pats some of the play dough into a pancake shape. Then she presses and rolls the coconut on the play dough and observes the impressions it makes. (If you have youngsters who are allergic to coconut, omit the flavoring and replace the coconut with a brown ball.)

Janet Boyce, Hinojosa Early Childhood and Pre-Kindergarten Center, Houston, TX

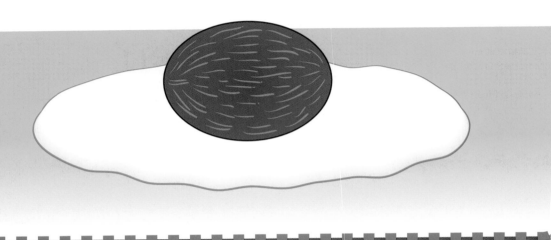

Rockin' Rhymes

Play a recording of lively music and invite youngsters to dance. Randomly stop the music and direct little ones to freeze. Say a word and point to a child. Prompt her to say a real or nonsense rhyming word. Then restart the music and play another round.

Tricia Kylene Brown
Bowling Green, KY

Busy Kids®

Fine- and Gross-Motor Activities for Developing Little Muscles and Big Muscles

Watch It Spin

Gather a collection of items that spin. You might consider using tops, toy vehicle wheels, small plastic bottles, plastic eggs, jar lids, milk jug caps, CDs, and toy rings. Youngsters attempt to spin the items, observing and determining which objects spin the fastest or which objects spin the longest.

Megan Taylor
Rowlett, TX

Climb the Ladder

Attach masking tape strips to the floor to create a ladder. Ask youngsters to pretend to be firefighters. Then name a movement and have each little firefighter use that movement to "climb" the ladder. Continue in this manner for a few more rounds. For the final round, invite each child to choose the movement she would like to use to climb the ladder.

Janet Boyce
Hinojosa Early Childhood and Pre-Kindergarten Center
Houston, TX

Pumpkin Bottles

Stuff lengths of white yarn (pumpkin guts) into a small, clear water bottle. Then hide a few pumpkin seeds among the strings. Place at a center the bottle and a pair of long tweezers. A child searches for the seeds by pulling out the guts with the tweezers. After he has found the seeds, he returns the guts and seeds to the bottle to ready the center for the next visitor.

Janet Boyce
Hinojosa Early Childhood and Pre-Kindergarten Center
Houston, TX

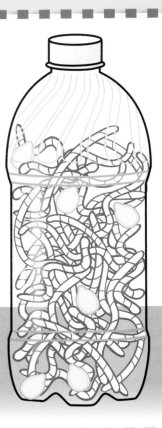

Fall Hayride

Place brown paper shreds (hay) in a wagon. Provide several stuffed toys or dolls and farmer-related clothing. A child puts on desired clothing. Then she helps a few toy passengers into the wagon and pulls them around the room for a fabulous hayride! For added fun, create a pumpkin patch by placing small pumpkins on a length of brown bulletin board paper. The farmer pulls the wagon to the pumpkin patch and helps each passenger pick a pumpkin.

Connie Taylor Barbier
Raceland Lower Elementary
Raceland, LA

Crop Transport

Set out several colors of play dough, a toy barn or barn cutout, and toy farm vehicles and wagons. A child uses the play dough to create a selection of crops. Then he uses the farm vehicles and wagons to transport the crops to the barn.

Janet Boyce
Hinojosa Early Childhood and Pre-Kindergarten Center
Houston, TX

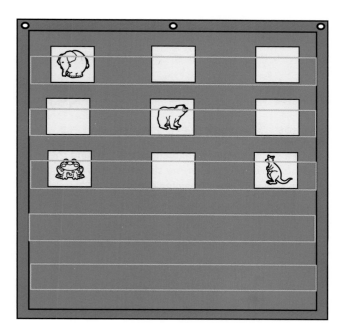

Gross motor

Choose and Move

Make several copies of the cards on page 43 so there is one card per student. Then place each card in a pocket chart so the blank sides are facing out. Put the pocket chart at one end of an open area. Have youngsters line up at the other end of the open area. In turn, each child walks to the pocket chart, turns over a card, and names the animal. Then he moves like that animal to get back to the group. Continue in this manner until each child has had a turn.

Amy Jastrzebski
Tender Care Learning Center—Jefferson
Clairton, PA

Busy Kids®

Fine- and Gross-Motor Activities for Developing Little Muscles and Big Muscles

Veggie Wash

Fill a clean tub with water and add a tiny squirt of dish soap. Provide a variety of vegetables, such as carrots, celery, broccoli, and cauliflower. Also provide clean sponges and brushes. Encourage youngsters to wash and scrub the vegetables. After students have had plenty of time to clean and explore the food, make sure it has been rinsed thoroughly. Then chop the vegetables and provide them as a snack for little ones with a healthy dip option!

Maggie Appel, Skidaddles, Mason, OH

Floppy, Floppy Scarecrows

Cut apart the cards on page 44 and place them in a gift bag. Have a child choose a card and then identify the body part on the card. Next, lead students in reciting the rhyme shown as they bend and flop the appropriate body part. Continue in the same way with the remaining cards.

The funny, funny scarecrow
Guards the fields all day.
It waves its floppy, floppy [arms]
To scare the crows away!

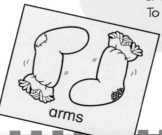
arms

head

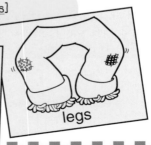
legs

Jingle Bell Bowling

'Tis the season for...bowling? You bet, when the bowling pins look and sound like Christmas! Make bowling pins by filling empty two-liter soda bottles with colorful materials such as pom-poms, crinkled gift bag shreds, or crumpled tissue paper. Then drop a few jingle bells into each bottle to add a festive sound. Hot-glue the lids onto the bottles. Set them up in a pyramid shape and provide a small ball. Invite each youngster to take a turn bowling over the pins. Then have the class count aloud the number of pins knocked down each time.

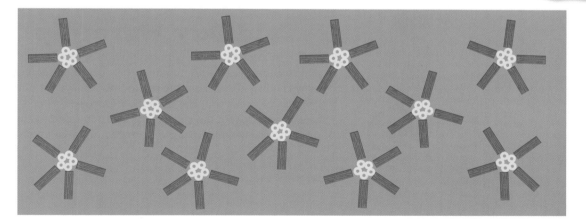

Poinsettia Sets

Youngsters make lovely poinsettias with this project! In advance, attach sets of five yellow hole reinforcers (or yellow hole-punch dots) to a length of green bulletin board paper. Provide lengths of red crepe paper streamer. A child cuts strips from the streamer and glues one next to each reinforcer so the strips resemble a poinsettia's red leaves. She continues with other sets of reinforcers.

Janet Boyce
Hinojosa Early Childhood and Pre-Kindergarten Center
Houston, TX

Gorgeous Garland

Suspend a jump rope in your classroom and set a supply of fabric strips nearby. Teach little ones how to tie the strips to the rope using a simple overhand knot. Then invite youngsters to visit the center and tie strips to the jump rope. What a great fine-motor workout!

Mary Davis, Keokuk Christian Academy, Keokuk, IA

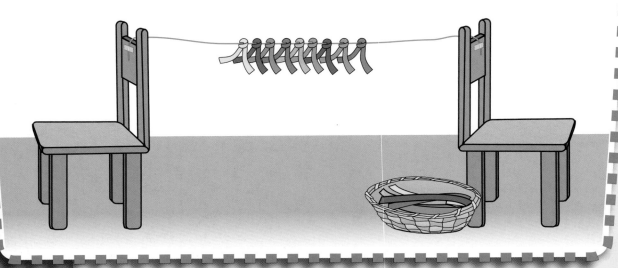

Cold Day Warm-Up

Ask youngsters to help you brainstorm a list of things that they can do to warm up on a chilly day. Then secretly tell a child an action from the list and have him act it out. Invite a volunteer to name the action. Once it is named, have the group join the child in acting it out. Continue for several more rounds, using a different action each time.

Tricia Kylene Brown
Bowling Green, KY

Busy Kids®

Fine- and Gross-Motor Activities for Developing Little Muscles and Big Muscles

Snowy I Spy

Partially fill a plastic jar with salt (snow) and hide several small erasers of various shapes in the snow. Secure the lid with tape. Next, prepare a checklist similar to the one shown and laminate it. Set out the container, the checklist, and a dry-erase marker. A child manipulates the container to find the erasers. As she finds each eraser, she checks it off the list. She continues until each eraser has been checked off.

Janet Boyce
Hinojosa Early Childhood and
    Pre-Kindergarten Center
Houston, TX

Dazzling Dancers

Personalize a card for each child. Then have him decorate his card with self-adhesive foam shapes and stickers. During circle time, hold up a card. The child whose name is on the card stands and dances as the rest of the group claps and sings the song shown. Continue in this manner with the remaining cards.

(sung to the tune of "The Farmer in the Dell")

> [Ben] is here today.
> [Ben] is here today.
> We all clap and say, "Hooray!"
> [Ben] is here today.

Janelle Johnson
Grand Forks, ND

Bird Food

Tape one end of a length of yarn to the inside of a shallow pan and then secure a plastic needle to the opposite end of the yarn. Place containers of low-sugar O-shaped cereal, slices of slightly stale bread, and plastic knives nearby. A child places a slice of bread in the pan and then cuts it into pieces. Next, she strings bread and cereal pieces on the yarn. Tie the ends of the yarn and then hang these treats outside for the birds to enjoy.

Janet Boyce
Hinojosa Early Childhood and Pre-Kindergarten Center
Houston, TX

Down the Path

Arrange several carpet squares or laminated sheets of construction paper to make a path. (If using laminated construction paper, tape each piece to the floor.) Place a large foam die at the beginning of the path. A child rolls the die and counts the number of dots. Then he picks up the die and takes a matching number of giant steps along the path. He continues in this manner until he gets to the end of the path.

Mary Hogan, Kidz Skool, Clifton Park, NY

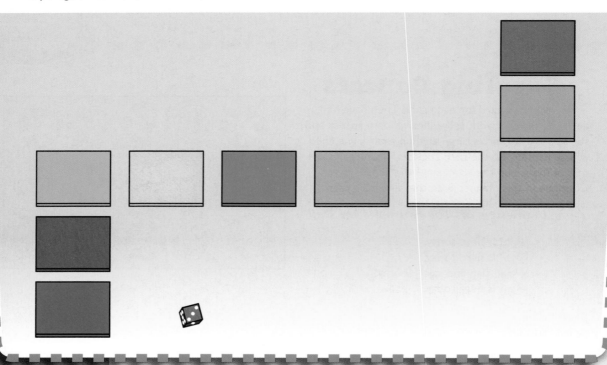

Shaving Cream Surprises

In each of several resealable plastic bags, squirt a generous amount of shaving cream. Place a small object in each bag so that it is covered by the shaving cream. Seal the bags and lay them flat in the freezer. Set out the frozen bags and a couple of pairs of gloves or mittens. A child puts on a pair of gloves or mittens and manipulates a bag to thaw the shaving cream and reveal the hidden item.

Janet Boyce, Hinojosa Early Childhood and Pre-Kindergarten Center, Houston, TX

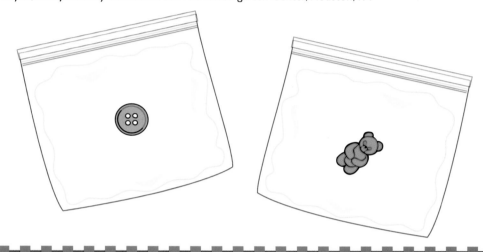

Jump or Glide

Use blue painter's tape to make two parallel lines a few feet apart on the floor. Have students pretend that this is a river and it's very cold and icy. Explain that they may either jump across the river or glide across the river. Then prompt students to take turns crossing the river using their desired method.

Kimberly Kratochvil
Mountainland Head Start
Provo, UT

Busy Kids®

Fine- and Gross-Motor Activities for Developing Little Muscles and Big Muscles

Gross motor

Pop!

Counting Pops

Get youngsters counting and jumping with this activity! Have students walk in a circle holding hands as you lead them in reciting the rhyme shown. When you're finished, prompt youngsters to stand still and release hands. Then say, "Give me one pop!" Prompt students to jump once and shout, "Pop!" Next, say, "Give me two pops!" and have students jump twice and shout, "Pop, pop!" Continue until youngsters reach ten pops. What fun!

One pop, two pops, three pops, four.
We turn up the heat and pop some more.
Five pops, six pops, seven pops, eight.
Hurry up popping. We can't be late!
Nine pops, ten pops, we're all done.
Popping our popcorn is lots of fun!

Margaret Aumen, Emory United Methodist Nursery School
New Oxford, PA

Fine motor

A Leprechaun Collection

Cut out a supply of leprechaun patterns (see page 45) and hide them around the room. Place a length of green bulletin board paper on a table and provide crayons and glue. Explain that the classroom has an infestation of leprechauns and that leprechauns can be very mischievous! Enlist youngsters' help in finding and securing all the leprechauns. During center time, a child searches for a leprechaun. When she finds one, she colors him as desired and then glues him to the paper. Soon the paper will be covered with captured leprechauns!

Tricia Kylene Brown, Bowling Green, KY

Little Lamb

Draw a lamb face on a small paper plate and then glue it to a sheet of green construction paper. To make the lamb's ears, round the corners of a 1" x 5" black paper strip and cut it in half. Glue the ears beside the lamb's face. Brush glue around and below the lamb's face and cover it with stretched cotton balls.

Janet Boyce, Hinojosa Early Childhood and Pre-Kindergarten Center, Houston, TX

Bouncing Shapes

Place a class supply of craft foam shapes on a parachute (or bed sheet). Have youngsters stand around the perimeter and then pick up the parachute. Lead them in reciting the chant shown, moving the parachute as indicated. After the chant, have each student find a shape. Then have her name her shape and toss it back onto the chute.

You move the shapes up.   *Raise the parachute.*
You move the shapes down.   *Lower the parachute.*
You move the shapes up.   *Raise the parachute.*
And then you move them round and round.   *Walk in a circle.*
First, we move them this way.   *Keep walking.*
Then we hold them way up high.   *Walk while holding up the parachute.*
And then we make them fly!   *Lower the parachute and then pop it up so the shapes fly off.*

Margaret Aumen
Emory United Methodist Nursery School
New Oxford, PA

Egg Toss

Arrange students into pairs and have them sit cross-legged facing each other so their knees touch. Give each pair of youngsters a plastic egg. Have little ones toss the egg back and forth to each other. Next, have each student take a tiny scoot backward. Then encourage them to once more toss the egg back and forth. Continue, until youngsters are several feet apart and have difficulty catching the eggs.

Janet Boyce
Hinojosa Early Childhood and Pre-Kindergarten Center
Houston, TX

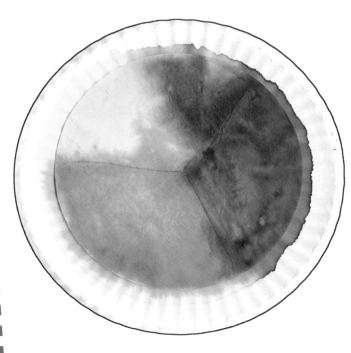

Color Combos

For each child, divide a coffee filter into thirds with light pencil lines. Provide red, yellow, and blue washable markers; paper plates (to protect the table surface); and a spray bottle of water. A child places a filter on a paper plate. Then she uses the markers to color each section a different color. Next, she mists the plate with water and watches as the colors blend to make secondary colors. Beautiful!

Janet Boyce

Busy Kids®

Fine- and Gross-Motor Activities for Developing Little Muscles and Big Muscles

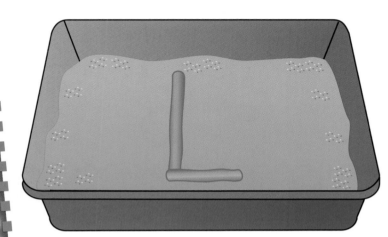

Mowing Letters

Put green sand or green-tinted rice in a tray to represent grass. Place a facedown stack of letter cards nearby. A child turns over a card and names the letter. Then she uses her finger to "mow" the grass to form the letter. (Mower sound effects make this particularly enjoyable!) She continues in this manner with other letters.

Tricia Kylene Brown
Bowling Green, KY

Sneaky Bunnies

Gather a plastic hoop (bunny hole) for each child in your class minus one. Choose one child to be the sleepy farmer. Tell the other students that they are sneaky bunnies that want to eat the vegetables in the farmer's garden. Direct each bunny to stand in a bunny hole. Invite the farmer to find a nice spot in his garden to "nap." As the farmer naps, the bunnies come out of their holes to wander around the garden. When the farmer wakes up, the bunnies quickly run back to their holes. Then choose a different child to be the farmer!

Kathy Reynolds
ACSU Early Education Program
Middlebury, VT

Unique Cutting Practice

Set out a few fun items that can be cut, such as play dough, clay, grass growing in flowerpots, and assorted cooked noodles. Also provide scissors. A child practices cutting these unique items!

Heather A. Eades
Sunnycrest Christian Academy
Golden, CO

Follow the Queen Bee

Wear a fun antenna headband and introduce yourself as the queen bee. Tell your little ones that they are the other bees that live in the hive and must follow all the directions that you give them. Have your little bees line up behind you. Then perform a variety of gross-motor movements, such as marching, hopping, tiptoeing, and crawling. Students will get a terrific gross-motor workout!

Tricia Kylene Brown
Bowling Green, KY

Water the Flowers

Place a row of large flower cutouts on the floor. Have youngsters stand in a line. Pass a watering can to the first child in line and invite her to quickly walk down the row of flowers, "watering" them, and repeat the process on the return trip. Then have her give the watering can to the next child and go to the back of the line. Little ones continue until everyone has had a turn watering the flowers. For extra fun, set a timer and have little ones see if they can beat the timer while playing a round of this game!

Elizabeth Cook, St. Louis, MO

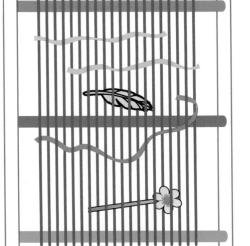

One-of-a-Kind Designs

Tie several lengths of yarn vertically around a ladderball game target, as shown. (You may wish to tape the yarn in place at the top and bottom of the frame.) Then place a basket of objects—such as lengths of ribbon, craft feathers and artificial flowers—nearby. A child creates a unique design by weaving the objects through the yarn.

Jodi and Linda Remington
Busy Day Child Care
Okemos, MI

Fun With Feathers

Here's additional fine-motor fun with a feather theme!

ideas contributed by Janet Boyce, Hinojosa Early Childhood and Pre-Kindergarten Center, Houston, TX

Bead, Bead, Straw...

Cut several colorful straws into one-inch pieces. Place the straw pieces in a bin along with preschool-appropriate stringing beads and feathers. A child pushes the feathers through the straws and beads.

Feathers All Around

Turn a muffin pan upside down and wrap a rubber band around the base of each cup. Place a container of colorful feathers nearby. A youngster places the feathers between the rubber bands and the cups. To include sorting practice in this activity, encourage her to group the feathers by color or size.

A Beautiful Bouquet

Turn a colander upside down and set a variety of colorful feathers nearby. A child pokes feathers into the holes to create a one-of-a-kind arrangement.

©The Mailbox®

©The Mailbox®

©The Mailbox®

©The Mailbox®

©The Mailbox®

©The Mailbox®

Picture Cards

Use with "Floppy, Floppy Scarecrows" on page 30.

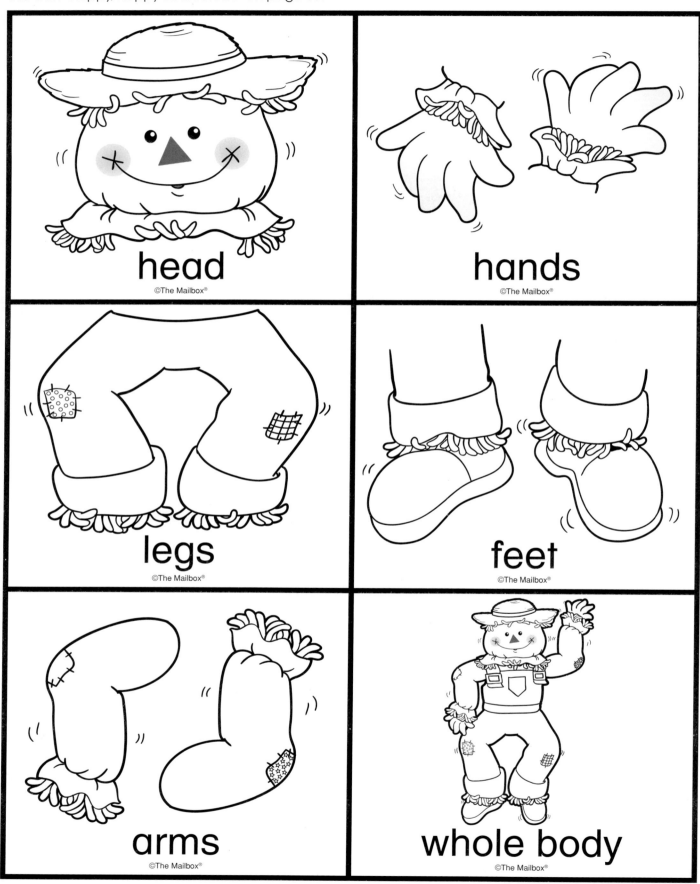

head
©The Mailbox®

hands
©The Mailbox®

legs
©The Mailbox®

feet
©The Mailbox®

arms
©The Mailbox®

whole body
©The Mailbox®

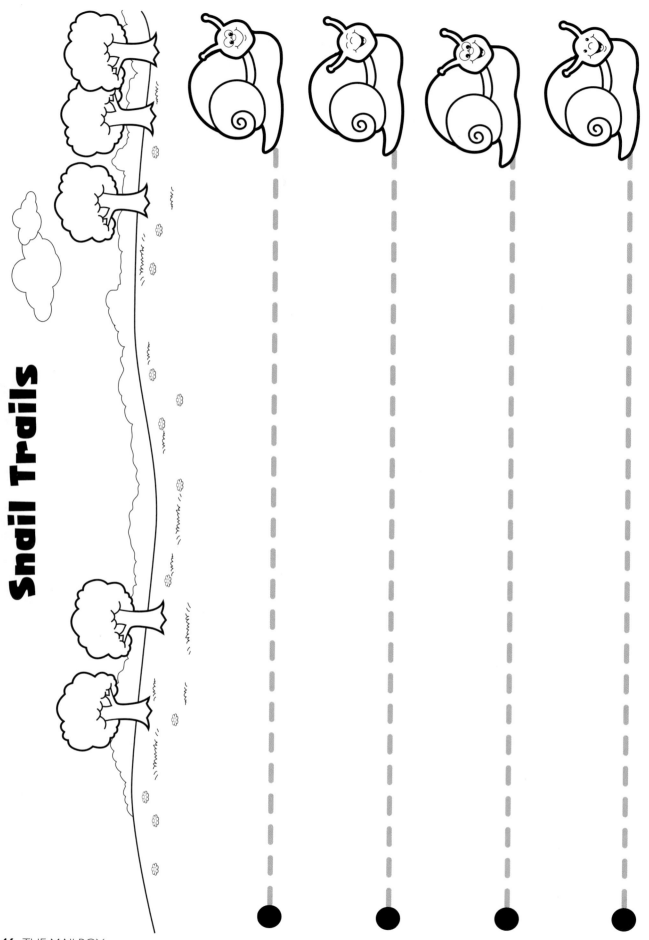

Snail Trails

©The Mailbox®

Note to the teacher: Have a child squeeze a line of glue along each dotted line. Then have him sprinkle colorful glitter on the glue. Next have him shake off the excess glitter and set his paper aside to dry.

A Valentine's Day Surprise

©The Mailbox®

Note to the teacher: Have each child use a red crayon to trace the heart. Then have her tear and crumple pieces of brown tissue to make chocolates. Direct her to glue the chocolates inside the outline of the heart.

Colorful Wings

Color.

Crumple.

Glue.

Note to the teacher: Have a child color the body of the butterfly. Then have her crumple squares of colorful tissue paper and glue them to the wings.

CIRCLE TIME

Circle Time

Bandanna Dance

Distinguishing right from left, gross-motor skills

This movement activity is perfect for helping youngsters distinguish between right and left. Tie a bandanna to each child's left arm and left leg. Then play a recording of upbeat music and invite youngsters to dance. As students dance, announce a direction that includes left or right, such as "Raise your left hand" or "Stomp your right foot." Each child incorporates the announced movement into his dance. Repeat this activity, varying the music and movements.

Andrea Moncrief
Beach Babies Childcare at Rehobeth
Rehobeth Beach, DE

Did You Ever See...?

Substituting beginning sounds

Watch your youngsters' smiles bloom with each verse of this silly song! Using magnetic letters, spell the word *sunflower* on a cookie sheet. Also have on hand a variety of consonant magnetic letters. Gather your little ones and teach them the song below. As you sing the word *sunflower*, point to the word on the cookie sheet. Then replace the S in *sunflower* with a different consonant and say the resulting word. During the next repetition of the song, sing the silly word in place of *sunflower*. Repeat this process several times for guaranteed fun!

(sung to the tune of
"Did You Ever See a Lassie?")

Did you ever see a sunflower,
A sunflower, a sunflower?
Did you ever see a sunflower?
It starts with /s/!

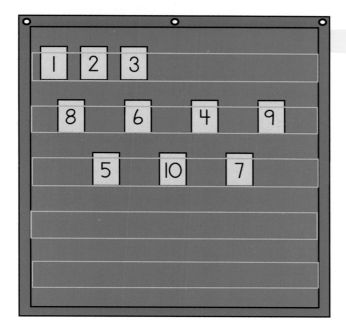

Next Number

Recognizing numbers, ordering numbers

Write each number from 1 to 10 on separate cards. Randomly place the cards in a pocket chart, leaving the top row empty. Invite a volunteer to find the card labeled "1" and place it in the top row. Then lead the group in saying the chant shown. At the end of the chant, ask a child to find the next number and place it in the top row of the chart. Continue until the number cards are in order.

Next number, next number,
Who can find the next number?

Margaret Aumen
Emory United Methodist Nursery School
New Oxford, PA

Look and Move

Recognizing shapes in the environment

Gather a collection of objects or pictures of objects that represent the following shapes: square, rectangle, circle, and triangle. Post large cutouts of the shapes on separate classroom walls. Display an object. Direct little ones to look at its shape and move to stand near the shape cutout represented by the object. Then show students a different object and have them move to the shape cutout represented by that object. Continue with the remaining objects.

Brooke Beverly
Dudley Elementary
Dudley, MA

Circle Time

Off to School

Recognizing one's own name

Color an enlarged copy of the bus pattern on page 65 and then attach the hook side of a strip of Velcro fastener to the bus. For each child, prepare a personalized craft stick like the ones shown. Then attach the loop side of a piece of Velcro fastener to the back of each stick. Post the bus and place the sticks nearby. Lead youngsters in singing the song. As you sing the song, the named child finds her stick and attaches it to the bus. Continue until each child's stick is on the bus.

(sung to the tune of "The Farmer in the Dell")

[Emily]'s on the bus.
[Emily]'s on the bus.
Heigh-ho, to school we go!
[Emily]'s on the bus.

Connie Childs-Massingill
Dawn til Dusk Daycare
Zionsville, IN

Take and Trace

Forming one's own name

Write each child's name on a sentence strip and laminate the strips. Hold up a strip and ask, "Whose name is this?" Give clues, if necessary. When a child recognizes her name, she takes her strip and gives you a high five. After all the names have been distributed, give each child a wipe-off marker and direct her to trace over the letters in her name.

Mary Beilke
Kid's Corner Preschool
Shoreview, MN

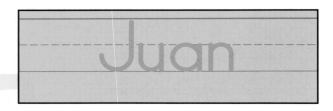

Color Search

Color recognition

Cut cards from colorful construction paper and place them in a small gift bag. Invite a volunteer to take a card from the bag and show it to his classmates. Then lead the group in singing the song shown. At the end of the song, direct each child to find an object of that color and stand next to it. After each child has found an object of the matching color, have him return to the circle time area for another round.

(sung to the tune of "Are You Sleeping?")

Where is [yellow]?
Where is [yellow]?
Do you see?
Do you see?
Can you show me [yellow]?
Can you show me [yellow]?
Please show me.
Please show me.

Karen Brown
Community Children's Center
Traverse City, MI

Katie   Jason   Grace

Disappearing Names

Recognizing one's own name

To make a wand, glue a jumbo pom-pom to the end of a large craft stick. Then write each child's name on your whiteboard. Pass the wand to a child. Invite him to find his name and then rub the wand over it to make it disappear. Continue until all the names have disappeared.

Mary Godin
Heart of the Valley YMCA
Kimberly, WI

 tip This idea also makes a terrific transition! After each child erases his name, have him move on to the next activity!

Circle Time

Five jumps.

Falling Leaves

Number recognition, counting, gross-motor skills

Use the leaf patterns on page 66 to create a class supply of leaf cutouts. Label the leaves with desired numbers. Have youngsters sit in a circle. Stand in the center of the circle and toss the leaves up and let them float to the ground. Invite each child to pick up a leaf and then return to her seat. Announce a number and an action. Youngsters whose leaves are labeled with that number stand and perform the named action a matching number of times. Play for several more rounds using different numbers and actions.

Katie Greenhaw
Growing Minds Learning Center
Fayetteville, GA

A Missing Pumpkin

Participating in a group activity

Have youngsters sit in a circle and then invite one child to be Peter. Ask Peter to stand in the center of the circle and cover his eyes. Have the seated students pass a small pumpkin around the circle as you lead them in saying the chant shown. At the end of the chant, direct the child holding the pumpkin to hide it behind his back. Next, Peter uncovers his eyes and tries to guess who has the pumpkin. After the child with the pumpkin is revealed, choose a different youngster to be Peter and play another round.

Peter, Peter, where's your pumpkin?
Somebody took it from your patch.
Guess who—it might be you.
Or it might be something that goes boo!

Becky Cook, Natural Choice Academy, Phoenix, AZ

Special Families

Naming family members, speaking to share information

Students share the names of family members with this cute activity. In advance, ask each child to bring a photo of his family. Then lead children in saying the rhyme shown. Next, invite each child to show his photo and say, "My family is" and then name each member of his family.

My family is special
'Cause it belongs to me!
Every family is different,
As you can plainly see.

Christine Vohs
College Church Preschool
Olathe, KS

Five Little Pilgrims

Participating in an action rhyme

Lead little ones in performing this action rhyme that helps them remember the Thanksgiving Day story.

There were five little pilgrims getting on the boat.	*Hold up five fingers.*
The first one said, "I hope it stays afloat."	*Shrug shoulders.*
The second one said, "I think I'm getting sick."	*Hold stomach and groan.*
The third one said, "Some rice will do the trick."	*Pretend to serve rice.*
The fourth one said, "This boat is really slow."	*Turn up palms.*
The fifth one said, "But we've got so far to go."	*Shade eyes and look around.*
Land-ho!	*Point.*
It's the end of our trip.	*Mop brow.*
And those five pilgrims said, "Get us off this ship!"	*Pretend to run off ship.*

Helen Agnew
Blessed Sacrament School
Walpole, MA

Circle Time

Follow the Sleigh

Tracking print

Have each child attach a profile photo of himself to a sleigh pattern (see page 67) and then tape the sleigh to a craft stick to make a pointer. Make a pointer for yourself as well. Write the lyrics to the song "Over the River and Through the Wood" on sentence strips. Place the strips in a pocket chart. Lead the group in singing the song as you use the pointer to track print, prompting students to hold their pointers in the air and track the print from left to right as well. Then invite a volunteer to be the "teacher" and track the print with his pointer on the chart. Be sure to leave student pointers near the chart for those who want to repeat the activity during center time!

Roxanne LaBell Dearman
NC Intervention for the Deaf and Hard of Hearing
Charlotte, NC

Alphabet Ornaments

Letter identification

Use a permanent marker to program each of 26 colorful plastic ornaments with a different letter of the alphabet or use the ornament patterns on page 67 to make a set of ornaments. Set a small undecorated tree and the ornaments in your circle time area. Invite a child to pick an ornament, name the letter, and then put the ornament on the tree. Continue until all the ornaments are on the tree.

Christine Vohs
College Church Preschool
Olathe, KS

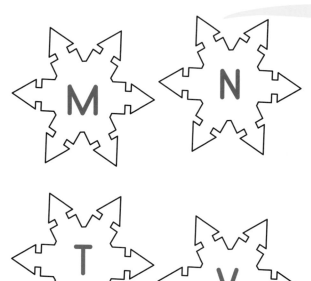

Falling Flakes

Symbol review

You can review desired skills with this fun snowflake game! Use the snowflake patterns from page 68 to prepare a class supply of snowflake cutouts. Laminate the snowflakes. Then use a wet-erase marker, such as a Vis-à-Vis marker, to program the snowflakes with shapes, letters, or numbers. Place them on a parachute (or bedsheet). Gather youngsters around the parachute. As you lead them in singing the song shown, have students lift the parachute to toss the snowflakes. At the end of the song, encourage each youngster to pick up a snowflake and identify the symbol on it.

(sung to the tune of "Are You Sleeping?")

Snowflakes falling.
Snowflakes falling
All around,
All around.
Falling softly—sh, sh!
Falling softly—sh, sh!
Pick one up
From the ground.

Susan Foulks, Carl A. Furr Elementary, Concord, NC

Hide-and-Seek Groundhogs

Positional words

Prior to Groundhog Day, have each child color a copy of the groundhog pattern on page 68. Before youngsters arrive on Groundhog Day, hide the groundhogs around the room. Explain to students that the groundhogs don't want to get out of their warm winter beds this morning and you need students' help to find them and wake them. Invite each child to find a groundhog and say, "Wake up, Mr. Groundhog." Then have him use positional words to identify his groundhog's hiding place.

Tricia Kylene Brown
Bowling Green, KY

Circle Time

Tooth Fairy Search

Color identification

Reinforce color identification with this cute idea. Make rectangle cutouts (pillows) in different colors. Then place them in a pocket chart. Secretly hide a tooth cutout behind one of the pillows and place a fairy wand near the pocket chart. Lead the group in saying the rhyme below. Then give the wand to a child and invite her to be the tooth fairy. Have her tap a pillow and name its color. Remove the pillow from the pocket chart. If the tooth is not there, pass the wand to a different child and continue until the tooth is found. If the tooth is behind the pillow, rehide the tooth and play another round.

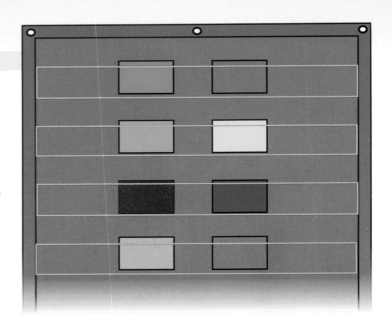

Tooth Fairy, Tooth Fairy,
Look and find
Which of these pillows
The tooth is behind.

Karen Smith, Little Tid-Bits, Fresno, CA

Special Delivery

Recognizing one's own name

Personalize a heart cutout for each child and place the hearts in a tote bag. Pretend to be a mail carrier driving a mail truck in the center of the circle as you lead students in saying the rhyme shown. At the end of the rhyme, take a few hearts from the bag. Hold up each one individually and encourage the owner to take his heart and place it in his mailbox or cubby. Continue until each child has a heart.

Here comes the mail carrier, driving down the street.
She has a truck that's really neat.
Maybe there's mail for you and me.
Stop the truck, and we can see!

Martha Lane, Weaver Elementary, Natchitoches, LA

tip > If you have a small class, you may want to play this game with one heart at a time, allowing the child whose heart is chosen to be the mail carrier for the next round.

Dancing Leprechauns

Participating in a song, gross-motor skills

Scatter shamrock cutouts on the floor. Then have students sit in a circle around the shamrocks. Choose two students to be leprechauns. Then lead youngsters in singing the song shown while the pair dances, twirls, hops, and then sits when indicated. Repeat the song several times with different student pairs!

(sung to the tune of "Six Little Ducks")

Little leprechauns I once knew
Danced in the shamrocks two by two.
First, they twirled, and then they hopped.
Then they quickly sat when the music stopped,
Music stopped, music stopped.
Then they quickly sat when the music stopped!

Spaghetti and Meatball Math

Developing addition and subtraction skills

Place white yarn (spaghetti) on a plate or platter. Then place a large supply of brown pom-poms (meatballs) on the yarn. Lead students in performing the rhyme shown several times. Then ask each child to estimate how many meatballs are on the plate. If desired, write down their estimates. Then lead youngsters in counting the meatballs and comparing the actual number to their estimates.

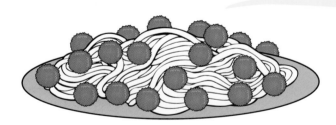

Spaghetti and meatballs, munch, munch, munch!
Spaghetti and meatballs for our lunch!
How many meatballs do you see?
Some for you and some for me!

Roll arms; then move hands like mouths.
Roll arms; then rub belly.
Throw arms outward.
Point to a classmate and then self.

Circle Time

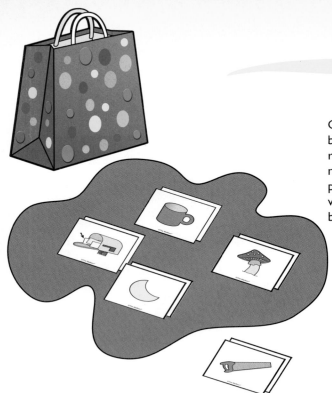

Splat!

Recognizing beginning sound /m/

Trim a piece of brown paper so it resembles a large mud puddle. Cut out a copy of the cards on page 69 and place them in a bag. To begin, have students sit around the mud puddle. Then have a child remove a card from the bag and name the picture. If the picture's name begins with /m/ like *mud*, the child drops the card in the mud puddle and everyone says, "Splat!" If the picture name doesn't begin with /m/, the child sets it aside. Continue until all the cards have been removed.

Where Are You, Little Chick?

Listening, participating in a game

Get a yellow pom-pom (chick). Choose one child to be the Mother Hen. Have the child close his eyes while a second child hides the chick. Next, have the Mother Hen open his eyes. Lead students in singing the song. Then prompt the Mother Hen to walk around the room as the remaining youngsters make cheeping noises. When the hen is closer to the chick, they cheep loudly and when he's far away, they cheep quietly. The game ends when the hen finds the chick.

(sung to the tune of "The Farmer in the Dell")

Cheep, cheep go the chicks
If the hen's not there.
Mother Hen protects her chicks.
They're with her everywhere.

Cindy Hoying
Centerville, OH

How Many Eggs?

Graphing

Gather a disposable bowl (nest) for each pair of youngsters in your class. Then put between one and four plastic eggs in each nest and hide the nests in the classroom. Display a floor graph with four columns and label the columns with numbers 1–4. To begin, pair students and then have each pair find a bird's nest and bring it back to the graph. Encourage each pair, in turn, to count the eggs in its nest and then place the nest in the appropriate column. When all the nests have been placed, have little ones compare the number of nests in the columns.

Roxanne LaBell Dearman
NC Intervention for the Deaf and Hard of Hearing
Charlotte, NC

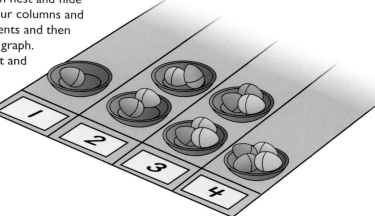

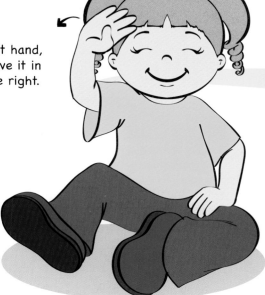

Hello
Position your right hand, as shown, and move it in a small arc to the right.

Hello, Friend!

Appreciating differences among people

Help develop student awareness that many people use American Sign Language to communicate. Begin by saying "Hello, friend" to each child in the circle. Then show youngsters how to sign "hello" and "friend" using American Sign Language. Finally, invite a volunteer to sign "Hello, friend" to another child in the group. Continue by giving other volunteers a turn greeting friends using American Sign Language.

Friend
Interlock your right and left index fingers and then repeat in reverse as shown.

Circle Time

Hop to Mr. Frog

Number recognition, counting, gross-motor skills

Combine math and movement with this fun activity. Have youngsters stand in a straight line on one side of your circle time area. Invite a child to be Mr. (or Miss) Frog and direct him to stand on the opposite side of the area facing the other students (little frogs). Have the little frogs say, "[Mr.] Frog, [Mr.] Frog, how many hops must we go?" Mr. Frog spins a spinner and announces the number. Each little frog hops that number of times. Continue until the little frogs reach Mr. or Miss Frog. Choose another child to be Mr. or Miss Frog and play another round.

Carole Watkins
Timothy Ball Elementary
Crown Point, IN

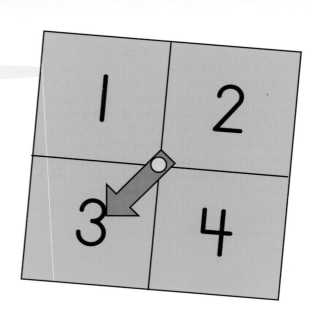

Catching Rhymes

Rhyming

Lead youngsters in singing the song shown. At the end of the song, have students act out tossing their lines in water. Then, in turn, have each child name a real or nonsense word that rhymes with *wish* and *fish* as she "reels" in her catch.

(sung to the tune of "Farmer in the Dell")

I wish to catch a fish.
I wish to catch a fish.
I grab my fishing pole.
I wish to catch a fish.

Cindy Hoying
Centerville, OH

Around the Circle

Naming the first letter of one's name

Students are sure to enjoy playing this literacy-themed version of Duck, Duck, Goose. Choose a child to be the duck. Direct her to say the alphabet as she waddles around the circle, touching each child's head. When she says the first letter of her name, she and the goose (the child whose head she last touched) waddle around the circle. Then the duck sits in the empty space in the circle. The goose becomes the duck, and play continues.

Peppy Sclafani
Kidspark Fresno
Fresno, CA

Build a Burger

Participating in a song

Students help Old MacDonald make the perfect burger during this entertaining song! Ask a child to name a topping that Old MacDonald might want on his burger. Then lead youngsters in singing the song shown, inserting the name of the topping where indicated. Sing additional verses using a different topping each time.

(sung to the tune of "Old MacDonald Had a Farm")

Old MacDonald had a burger.
E-I-E-I-O.
And on this burger he had some [cheese].
E-I-E-I-O.
With some [cheese] here,
And some [cheese] there.
Here some [cheese]. There some [cheese].
Everywhere some [cheese], [cheese].
Old MacDonald had a burger.
E-I-E-I-O.

Susan E. Tvedten
Bernie's Montessori School and Child Care
Richfield, MN

Circle Time

Pocket Chart Poem

Sequencing events

Color and cut apart a copy of the sequencing cards on page 70 and place them at the bottom of the pocket chart. Teach students the poem shown. Then have them help you arrange the pictures at the top of the chart to show the sequence of events.

I put on my rain boots.
I put on my hat.
I put on my raincoat just like that.

My umbrella goes up.
I run out to play.
The sun peeks out, and the rain goes away.

Cindy Hoying
Centerville, OH

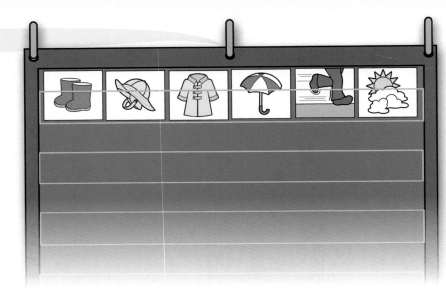

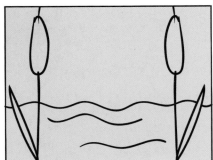

Buggy Homes

Exploring living things

Little ones explore the habitats of bugs with this activity. Gather plastic bugs—such as bees, dragonflies, and spiders—and place them in a paper bag. On separate sheets of construction paper, draw a habitat for each chosen bug. Invite each child to take a bug from the bag. Then show students one of the habitats and place it in the center of the circle time area. Ask each child who has a bug that would live in that habitat to place it on the drawing. Repeat this process with the other habitats. After all the bugs are on the correct habitat, guide youngsters to discuss why each bug lives where it does.

Debbie Wallbank
Edmonton, Alberta, Canada

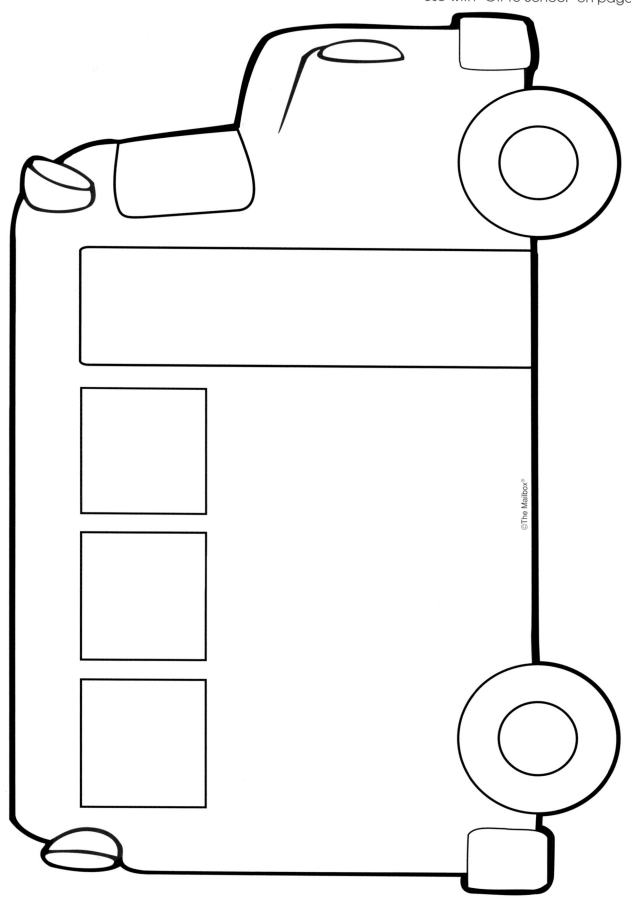

©The Mailbox®

Leaf Patterns
Use with "Swirl and Sway" on page 45 and "Falling Leaves" on page 54.

©The Mailbox®

©The Mailbox®

Sleigh Pattern
Use with "Follow the Sleigh" on page 56.

©The Mailbox®

Ornament Patterns
Use with "Alphabet Ornaments" on page 56.

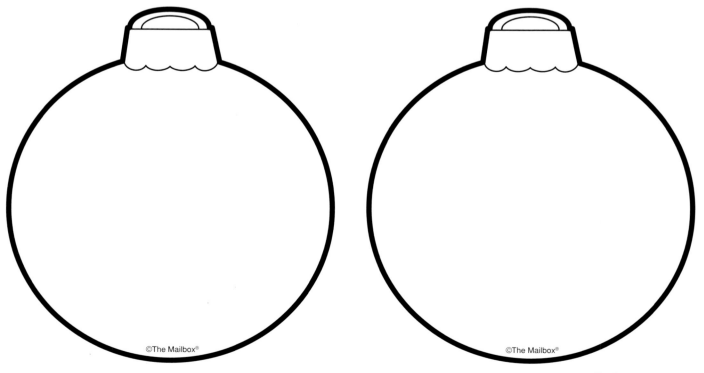

©The Mailbox®   ©The Mailbox®

Snowflake Patterns
Use with "Falling Flakes" on page 57.

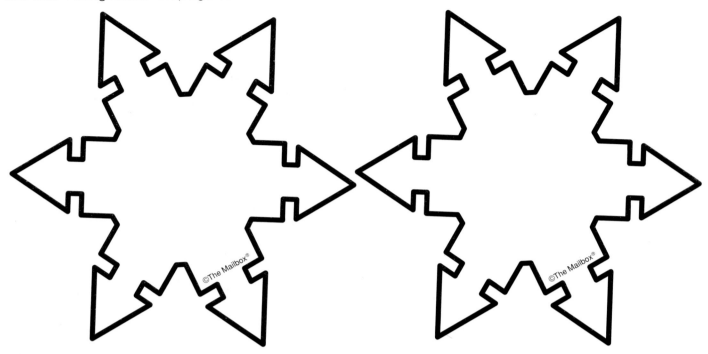

Groundhog Pattern
Use with "Hide-and-Seek Groundhogs" on page 57.

©The Mailbox®

©The Mailbox®

©The Mailbox®

©The Mailbox®

©The Mailbox®

©The Mailbox®

©The Mailbox®

©The Mailbox®

©The Mailbox®

©The Mailbox®

©The Mailbox®

©The Mailbox®

Sequencing Cards
Use with "Pocket Chart Poem" on page 64.

©The Mailbox®

©The Mailbox®

©The Mailbox®

©The Mailbox®

©The Mailbox®

©The Mailbox®

CLASSROOM DISPLAYS

CLASSROOM DISPLAYS

Dandelion Wishes

Encourage writing skills with this adorable display! Have each child paint a green stem and leaves on a sheet of paper. Then encourage her to sponge paint a circle above the stem so it resembles a dandelion that has gone to seed. For extra fun, have her sprinkle white glitter on the dandelion. Next, prompt her to dictate what wish she would make if she blew on a dandelion. Write her words on a piece of paper and attach it to the project. Then mount the projects as shown.

Teresa Wensil
Tiny Tears Daycare
Albemarle, NC

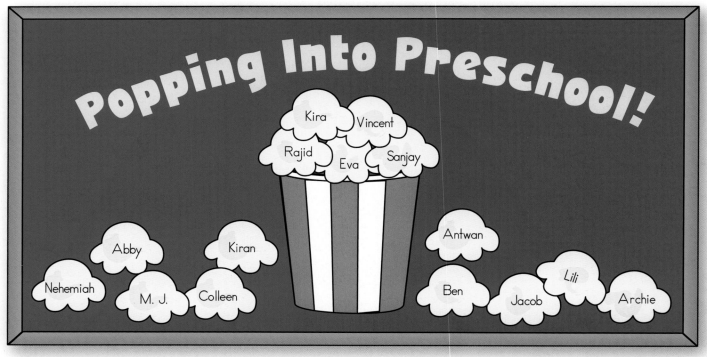

Make a simple poster board popcorn bucket as shown and attach it to a wall. Next, give each child a personalized white construction paper popcorn cutout (patterns on page 78). Have her use yellow watercolors (butter) to paint the cutout. Then attach it above and around the bucket. Add the title shown.

Megan Taylor, Rowlett, TX

Our Family Tree

With a few simple changes and the variations below, this tree can be displayed all year! Post a bare tree cutout and add green leaf cutouts. Snap a photo of each youngster with his family. Trim the photos and glue each one to a separate apple cutout. Invite each student to share his photo with the class. Then help him attach his apple to the tree.

 ## Variations

Pumpkin, Pumpkin

- **Falling for Great Books**
  Invite youngsters to use fall colors to sponge-paint a supply of leaf cutouts. Place the leaves near the board. After you read a book aloud, write the book's title on a leaf and post it on the tree.

- **Winter Wonderland**
  Invite each child, in turn, to share her favorite winter activity as you record her response on a snowflake cutout. Post the programmed flakes around the bare tree cutout.

- **Spring Has Sprung**
  Add green leaf cutouts to the tree. Invite each child to make a blossom; then help him display it on the tree.

- **We've Been Busy Bees!**
  For a year-end display, label a bee cutout with each child's name. Have each child dictate her favorite activity from the past school year as you write it on her cutout. Post the bees around the leafy tree.

CLASSROOM DISPLAYS

A Gorgeous Gobbler

This turkey display has a cooperative twist! Cut several large feathers from white poster board. Give each feather to a small group of students. In each small group, invite each child to choose a color of paint. Squirt the chosen colors of paint on the feather and direct youngsters to fingerpaint to cover it. Set the feathers from all the groups aside to dry. Display them behind a jumbo turkey body on a board titled as shown. *Cooperation*

Linda Wittmann, Faith Lutheran Preschool, Lincoln, NE

Attach twisted brown butcher paper to a bulletin board so it resembles a cave opening. Add cotton balls (snow) and the title shown. Have each child paint a small paper plate brown. Then have him color and cut out bear ears and a muzzle (patterns on page 79) and glue them to the plate. Next, direct him to add eyes with a crayon. Add the bears to the display along with bear facts dictated by the students and written on index cards. *Investigating living things*

Megan Taylor, Rowlett, TX

CLASSROOM DISPLAYS

The Jackets We Wear in the Snow!

Read aloud the book *The Jacket I Wear in the Snow* by Shirley Neitzel. Next, take a photo of each child in her jacket. Help her cut out the photo and then glue it to a copy of the snow globe pattern on page 80. Next, have her describe her jacket. Write her words on the base of the snow globe. Then have her color the globe and add iridescent glitter (snow). When the projects are dry, cut them out and mount them as shown.

Megan Taylor, Rowlett, TX

yellow
warm
puffy

A Lovely Garden

Send home a pink construction paper circle for each student and have parents write on it, describing what they love about their preschooler. Then have them send the circle back to school by a certain date. Read each circle to the appropriate child and then have the child glue red heart cutouts (petals), a green strip of paper (stem), and leaf cutouts to make a flower. Display the flowers as shown.

Kim Montanye, Glyndon United Methodist Preschool, Glyndon, MD

CLASSROOM DISPLAYS

Youngsters work with two different attributes with this display! Copy the transportation cards on page 81 on several colors of construction paper. Cut out the cards and randomly post them on a board. Repeat the chant "I spy with my little eye [a red car]," inserting a different color and mode of transportation each time. After ending each chant, invite youngsters to look on the board for the match.

These "hoppy" little "chocolate" bunnies look great displayed with a fun title! Help youngsters round two corners of a 9" x 12" sheet of construction paper to make the bunny's body. Give her two 3" x 9" strips of paper (ears). Have her round two corners of each ear and glue the ears to the body. Have her glue a belly cutout and inner ear cutouts made from patterned scrapbook paper and two brown semicircle paws to the project. Then encourage her to glue on facial feature cutouts. Mount the rabbits with the title shown. Adorable!

Megan Taylor, Oak Leaf Kids Academy, Rowlett, TX

CLASSROOM DISPLAYS

Muddy Madness!

For this marvelous and muddy display, have each child fingerpaint a mud puddle on a sheet of green paper. Next, take a photo of her with her messy fingers. Cut out a copy of the photo and glue it to her mud puddle painting. Then display the projects with the title shown!

Emily Mcdowell
H.E.L.P. For Mom Daycare and Preschool
Lebanon, IL

DIVING INTO SUMMER

Invite each child to use craft supplies to decorate a snorkeler cutout (pattern on page 82) so it resembles herself. Help each child write her name on her completed project; then post the projects on a board. Add lengths of twisted green crepe paper (seaweed) to complete the display.

Popcorn Patterns
Use with "Popping into Preschool" on page 72.

©The Mailbox®

©The Mailbox®

Snow Globe Pattern

Use with "The Jackets We Wear in the Snow!" on page 75.

©The Mailbox®

©The Mailbox®

©The Mailbox®

©The Mailbox®

©The Mailbox®

©The Mailbox®

Snorkeler Pattern
Use with "Diving Into Summer" on page 77.

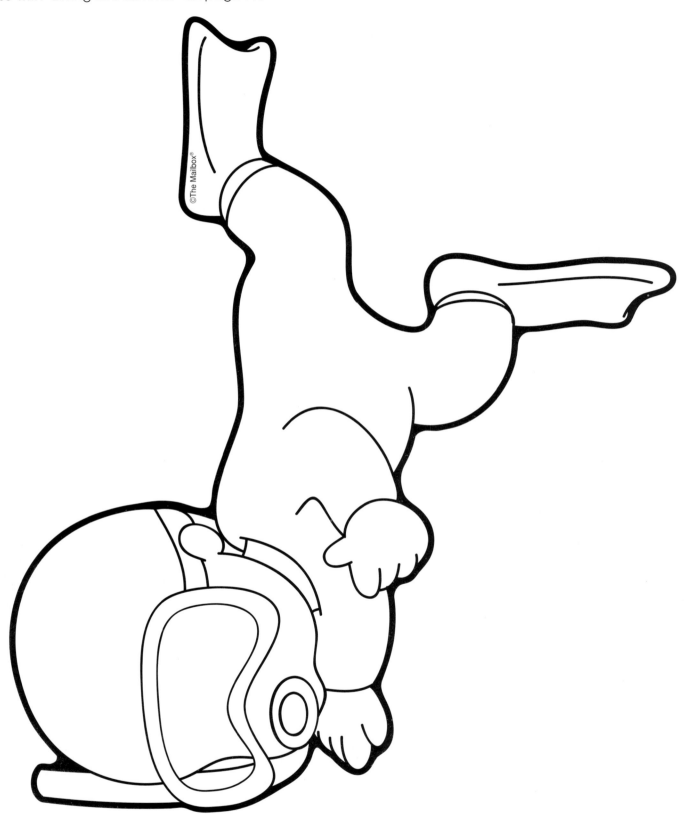

©The Mailbox®

HOLIDAYS & SEASONAL CELEBRATIONS®

& Seasonal Celebrations®

Ripening Apples

Investigating seasonal changes

It's September, and that means it's time for ripe apples! Give each child a green apple cutout. Explain that baby apples are green in the summertime but, when fall gets closer, they ripen and may turn red. Next, have each child "ripen" his apple by painting it red. As youngsters are painting, ask them to name some favorite apple treats!

Cori Marinan
Howe School
Green Bay, WI

Nutty Nut Count

Identifying numbers, counting

Place artificial or real fall leaves in your sensory table along with brown pom-poms (nuts). Label small plastic containers with different numbers. (Depending on your youngsters, you may wish to add a matching dot set to each label.) For extra fun, display a photo of a squirrel or place a stuffed toy squirrel at this center. Invite a child to the center and encourage him to identify a number, find that many nuts, and place them in the container. Have him continue for each container.

Dina Breckheimer
Hosanna! Preschool
Lakeville, MN

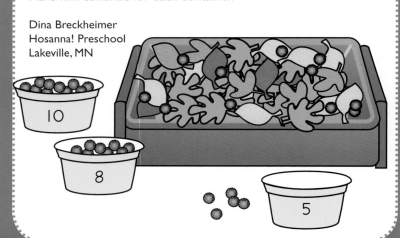

Here's a Little Pumpkin!

Little ones are sure to want repeat performances of this action rhyme!

Here's a little pumpkin.	*Make a circle with thumb and finger.*
Here's a bigger one too.	*Make a circle with hands.*
Here's a great big pumpkin	*Make a circle with arms.*
Just for you!	*Point to a classmate.*
I kept the little pumpkin.	*Make a circle with thumb and finger.*
I kept the bigger one too.	*Make a circle with hands.*
But I saved the biggest pumpkin	*Make a circle with arms.*
Just for you!	*Point to a classmate.*

Holidays & Seasonal Celebrations®

The Hibernation Dance!

Investigating animals

Some bears begin their hibernation in late November or early December and occasionally wake up throughout their long sleep. Reinforce this information with a very special dance! Play music and have youngsters dance around. Then stop the music and prompt little ones to gently fall to the floor and pretend to hibernate. After several moments of restful sleep, begin the music again and encourage students to dance. Play several rounds of this fun game.

Keely Saunders
Bonney Lake Early Childhood Education and Assistance
    Program
Bonney Lake, WA

A Class Gift

Predicting, participating in a game

'Tis the season for gift giving! Get a gift that the whole class will enjoy, such as a special DVD to watch or a tasty treat. Place the gift in a box and wrap the box. Then attach one bow for each child in the class. Give the gift to a child and encourage him to guess what he thinks might be in the box. Then have him remove a bow and give the gift to a classmate. Continue until each child has guessed and removed a bow. Then remove the paper and reveal the gift!

Amber Dingman
Play 'n' Learn Family Child Care and Preschool
Sterling, MI

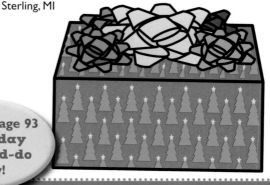

Check out page 93 for a **holiday listen-and-do** activity!

Let's Talk About Corn

Descriptive language

Use a decorative Thanksgiving Day item, Indian corn, as the focus of this idea. Show youngsters an ear of Indian corn and say a few words to describe it. Encourage little ones to add their own descriptions. Then play some lively music and direct students to pass the corn around the circle. Periodically stop the music and invite the child holding the corn to say a word or phrase to describe it. Continue the activity until each child has had a chance to practice using some descriptive language.

Thanksgiving Dinner

Dara is thankful.

See pages 96–98 for an awesome **Thanksgiving Day** booklet!

Holidays
& Seasonal Celebrations®

Hot Cocoa Exploration

Exploring volume, role playing

Hot cocoa is a favorite winter weather warm-up! For this hot cocoa–themed center, mix flour, salt, and hot cocoa mix in a tub and place it at a center along with measuring cups and drinking cups in different sizes. Also provide white pom-poms (marshmallows). Youngsters use the cups to scoop and explore the mix, noticing how the different cups hold different amounts. Then they "serve" hot cocoa to their friends!

Kelly Craven
Discovery Point
Dacula, GA

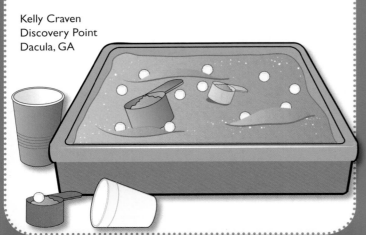

Counting Clover

Developing subtraction skills

Groundhog Day is February 2! Celebrate by teaching little ones a bit about groundhogs. In advance, glue wiggle eyes, a brown pom-pom nose, and brown felt ears to a brown sock to make a groundhog puppet. Cut five clover shapes from felt and place them on a flannelboard (or on the floor). Explain that groundhogs eat clover. Have a child put the sock puppet on her hand. Then lead students in reciting the rhyme shown, encouraging the groundhog puppet to "eat" one piece of clover when indicated. Continue until all the clover has been eaten. Then repeat the activity with a different youngster.

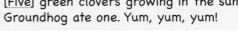

[Five] green clovers growing in the sun.
Groundhog ate one. Yum, yum, yum!

A Valentine Vase

Associating V with /v/

This V-shaped vase looks lovely holding a bouquet of valentines! Obtain three small valentines for each child. To begin, give each student a large *V* cutout and encourage him to glue it to a 12" x 18" sheet of construction paper in a contrasting color. Have each student trace the letter with his finger as he says its name. Next, have him glue three green construction paper strips (stems) inside the *V* as shown. Encourage him to glue a valentine at the top of each stem. Then have him glue green heart-shaped leaves to the stems. Explain that the words *valentine* and *vase* both begin with the letter *V*. Encourage students to say the words and exaggerate the /v/ sound. Finally, attach these lovely valentine vases to a bulletin board for a display that's simply smashing!

Let It Snow!

What Is Snow?

Building on background knowledge

Youngsters may not understand the scientific definition of *snow*—"precipitation in the form of small white ice crystals formed from water vapor at a temperature of less than 32°F"—but they do have definite ideas about what snow is! To find out what your students know about snow, divide a sheet of chart paper into three columns. Label each column with the heading "Snow Looks," "Snow Feels," or "Other Words About Snow." Then encourage youngsters to describe some things about snow. Ask them to decide in which column each of their descriptions fit. Youngsters might say the snow *looks* "white," "pretty," and "shiny" or *feels* "cold," "wet," and "crunchy." They might use words such as "falls," "melts," and "blows" for the last column of the chart. After completing the chart, share some of these snow facts with students.

- All snowflakes have six sides.
- Snowflakes fall in many different sizes and shapes.
- When snow melts, it becomes water.
- Snow helps protect plants and hibernating animals from the winter cold.

Snow Looks	Snow Feels	Other Words About Snow
white	cold	falls
pretty	wet	melts
shiny	crunchy	blows

Foil Flakes

Developing fine-motor skills

This sparkly art will be popular with your little ones! Place strips of foil at your art center along with sequins and blue, purple, or black construction paper. Have a child choose a sheet of construction paper. Next, have her glue strips of foil to the paper in sets of three so they resemble snowflakes. (To help youngsters understand, tell them to glue one strip up and down and then make an X with the two remaining strips.) Then have her add extra sparkle to the page with sequins.

Deborah J. Ryan, Newberg, OR

 Check out the snowman booklet on pages 99–101.

What to Wear?

Reinforcing seasonal characteristics, participating in a song

Guide students in naming different items of clothing they need to wear in cold weather. Write their ideas on chart paper. Then lead them in singing the song shown. Continue with several verses, naming a different item each time.

(sung to the tune of "When the Saints Go Marching In")

When winter comes,
The cold wind blows.
The sky turns gray, and then it snows.
Oh, I need to wear my [mittens]
When the cold wind starts to blow.

Suzanne Moore
Tucson, AZ

mittens
scarf
snowsuit
boots
coat
hat
gloves
sweater

Holidays

& Seasonal Celebrations®

Explore the Gold

Sorting, counting

Gather a large supply of medium-size rocks and spray-paint them gold. Then place them in a black plastic pot. (Hint: use a plastic Halloween cauldron or a plastic houseplant pot.) Put the resulting pot of gold at a center. Then encourage students to empty the pot and sort and count the gold as desired.

Deborah Provencher
West Brookfield Elementary
West Brookfield, MA

Eggs for Easter

Lead students in holding up their fingers to represent bunnies for this cute fingerplay!

Five little bunnies hop, hop, hop!
The first one said, "Is it time to stop?"
The second one said, "It's getting late!"
The third one said, "We have eggs to decorate."
The fourth one said, "Let's go, go, go!"
The fifth one said, "We can't be slow."
So the five little bunnies hopped away
To get their eggs ready for Easter day!

adapted from an idea by Kris Duncan
Children's Development Connection, Omaha, NE

A Brand-New Kite

Increasing print awareness, early writing

Take students' understanding of print concepts to new heights with this picture-perfect project! In advance, take a photograph of each youngster posed as if he is holding a kite string. Give each child a copy of a small kite pattern and a copy of the poem shown (patterns on page 90). Have him color the kite and cut it out. Working with one child at a time, read the poem and help the child write his dictated response on the blank line. Then assist each youngster in taping the poem, kite, and string to the photo as shown. Invite little ones to share their poems with the class. Display these high-flying projects for all to see!

 See **pages 102–103** for a **rainbow booklet.**

I flew my brand-new kite one day.
It went so very high.
It flew all the way to _Grandma's house_
As it sailed off into the sky!

Holidays
& Seasonal Celebrations®

Lovely Flowers

Developing fine-motor skills

Here's a Mother's Day gift that is sure to be popular! Have each child paint a craft stick green and make a colorful handprint on a sheet of paper. Also have her add dots to a small clay pot using bingo daubers. When the paint is dry, help her cut out the handprint and glue a circular photo of herself to the center. Instruct her to glue the handprint along with leaf cutouts to the stick so the project looks like a tulip. Next, have her press floral foam into the clay pot. Prompt her to push the tulip into the foam and then glue moss around the tulip. Finally, write "Happy Mother's Day" on the pot.

Sue Varallo
Annunciation Regional School
Bellmawr, NJ

A Father's Day Sing-Along!

Participating in a song

Invite fathers and other special male family members to the classroom for a Doughnuts With Dad celebration! Then have youngsters celebrate these special individuals with this catchy song.

(sung to the tune of "Are You Sleeping?")

I am lucky, I am lucky
To have you, to have you,
To have you to love me,
Help me, and encourage me.
I love you, I love you!

Virginia Latyak
Little Seedlings Preschool and Kindergarten
Leonardtown, MD

A Shapely Picnic

Matching shapes, shapes in the environment

Summertime is the perfect time for a picnic! Use a different-colored marker to draw a circle, square, or triangle on each of three paper plates. Also color and cut out a copy of the picnic foods on pages 91 and 92. Store the cutouts and plates in a picnic basket along with a blanket or plastic tablecloth. A child spreads out the blanket and then sorts each food cutout onto the plate with the corresponding shape.

See **pages 104–106** for a **summer booklet.**

Kite Pattern and Poem Card
Use with "A Brand-New Kite" on page 88.

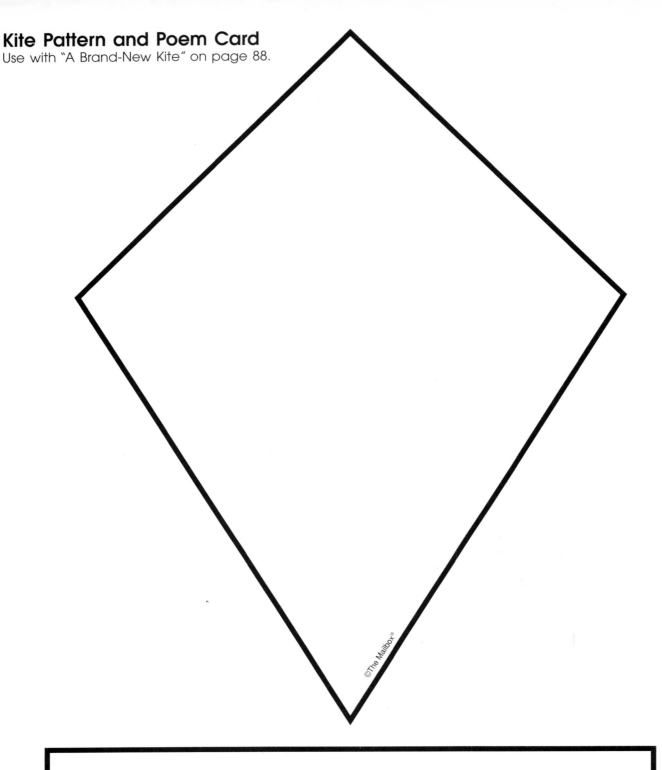

©The Mailbox®

I flew my brand-new kite one day.

It went so very high.

It flew all the way to _____

As it sailed off into the sky.

©The Mailbox®

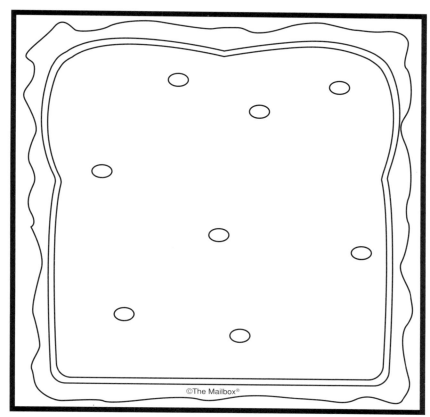

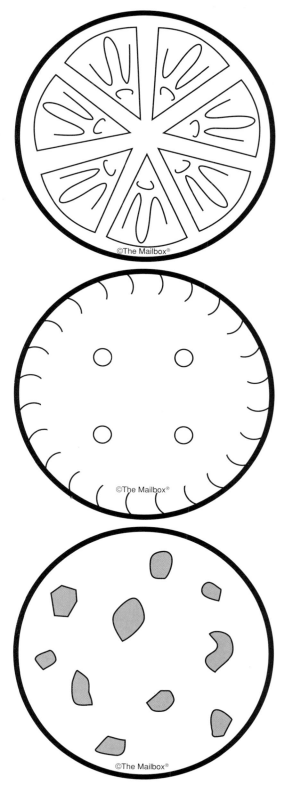

Chips

Picnic Food Patterns

Use with "A Shapely Picnic" on page 89.

Juice

©The Mailbox®

©The Mailbox®

©The Mailbox®

©The Mailbox®

Kitty's Christmas Cookies

Listen for directions.

Directions 1) Draw a face and buttons on the gingerbread man cookie. 2) Color the tree on the bag green. Draw decorations on the tree. 3) Draw red stripes on the candy cane-shaped cookie. 4) Draw sprinkles on the star-shaped cookie.

If I were a leprechaun, I would hide my gold...

Note to the teacher: Give a child a copy of this page. Have him dictate to complete the sentence. Then have him draw a picture to illustrate his words.

Bunny Buggy

Trace.

Thanksgiving Day Booklet

Make a copy of pages 96–98 for each child. Help her follow the directions for each booklet page. Then help her cut out and stack the pages, placing the cover on top. Staple the cover and pages to the booklet backing.

Cover and booklet page 1: Color the cover. Press the eraser end of a pencil in green paint. Then make green dots on the first page so they resemble peas.

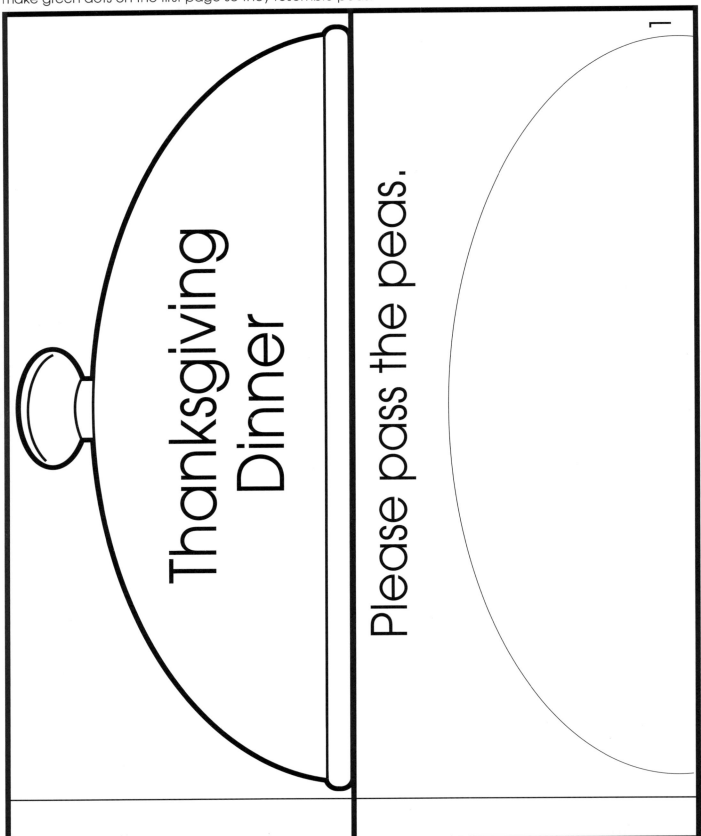

Booklet pages 2 and 3: Glue stretched cotton balls (mashed potatoes) to the dish on page 2. Then glue a yellow square (pat of butter) to the potatoes. Tear an oval shape from brown construction paper. Glue it to the dish on page 3. Then draw a bone next to the oval so it resembles a drumstick.

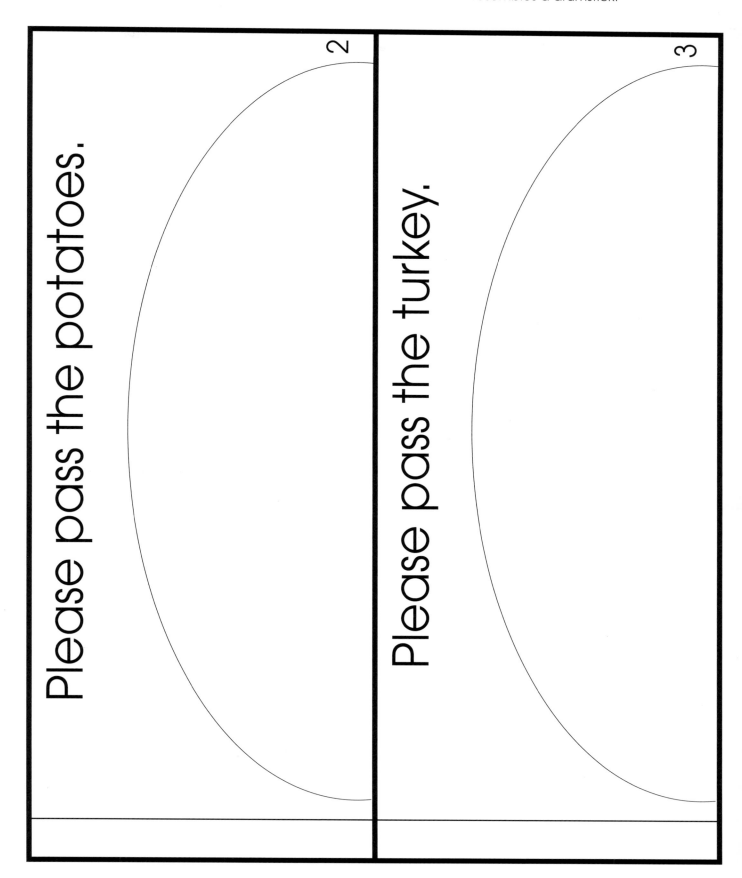

2

Please pass the potatoes.

3

Please pass the turkey.

Booklet backing: Dictate a type of food to be written in the top blank. Draw a picture of the food. Then write your name on the remaining blank.

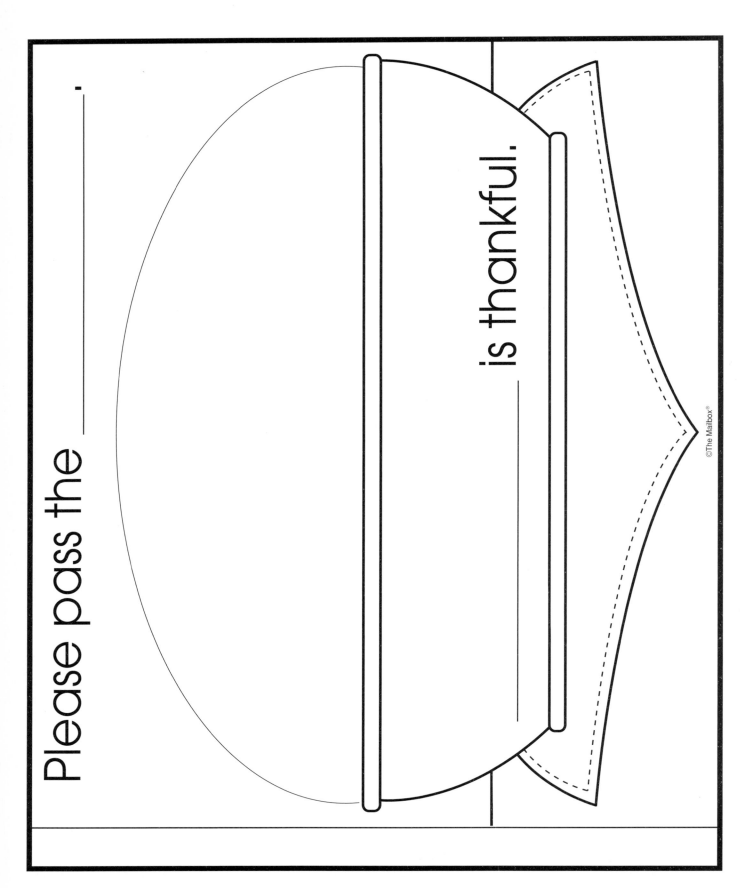

Please pass the _____.

_____ is thankful.

©The Mailbox®

Snowman Booklet: Cut out a copy of the booklet cover and booklet pages 1 and 2 on page 100 and booklet pages 3–5 on page 101. Stack the pages behind the cover and staple them to a copy of the booklet backing (booklet page 6) below. Next, read through the booklet and have the child trace the snowballs, add a face, and glue a fabric scrap hat to the snowman when indicated.

Staple here.

And that is that!

6

Building a Snowman

by _____

©The Mailbox®

Roll a large ⬤.

1

Roll a medium ⬤.

2

©The Mailbox®

Roll a small .

3

Make a .

4

Add a .

5

Rainbow Booklet

Make a copy of pages 102 and 103 for each child. Help her follow the directions for each booklet page. Then help her cut out the pages and staple them together.

Cover and Page 1: Color the cover and write your name in the space provided. Use blue watercolors to paint the rain on page 1.

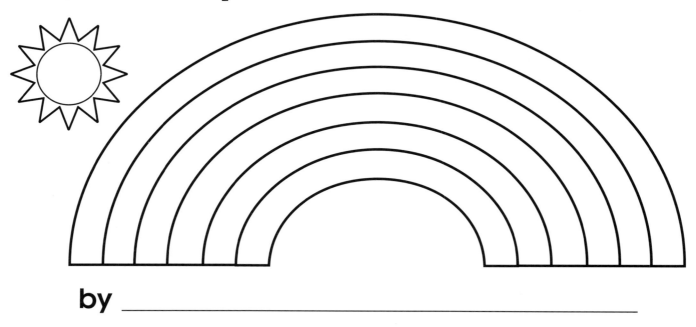

Recipe for a Rainbow

by _____

Rain.

1

Booklet Pages 2 and 3: For page 2, use a crayon to color the sun and its rays. Paint over the page with blue watercolors (rain). For page 3, color the sun and the rainbow. Then paint over the page with blue watercolors (rain).

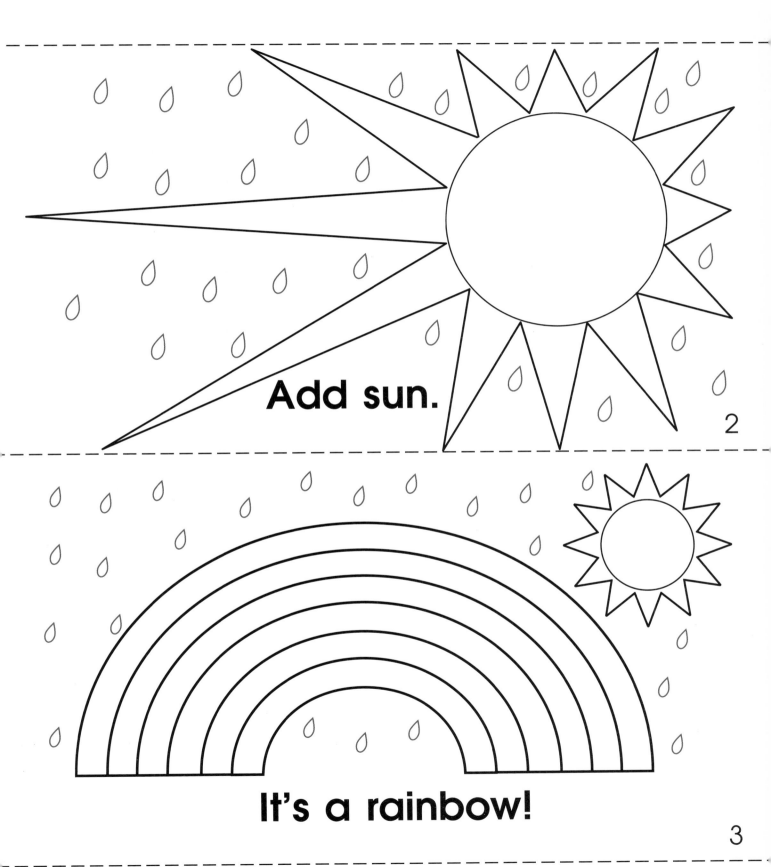

Add sun.

2

It's a rainbow!

3

Summer Booklet

Make a copy of pages 104–106 for each child. Help her follow the directions for the cover and each booklet page. Then help her cut out the pages, stack them in order behind the cover, and staple the project to make a booklet.

Cover and booklet page 1: Color the cover and page 1. If desired, glue green paper shreds to page 1 so they resemble grass.

I
See
Summer!

by _____

I see bare feet.

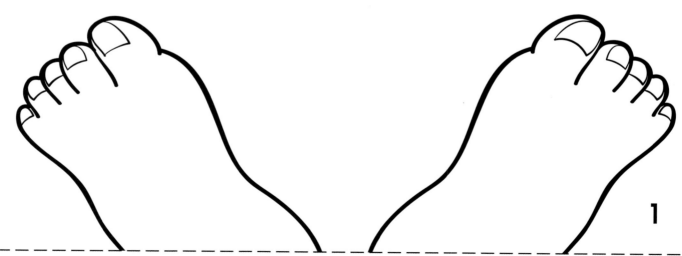

1

Booklet pages 2 and 3: Glue two white tissue paper squares (ice cubes) to the lemonade. Then use watercolors to paint the lemonade yellow. Color the fireflies yellow and the sky black. For an added touch, put a dot of glue on each firefly and then sprinkle gold glitter on the glue.

I see lemonade.

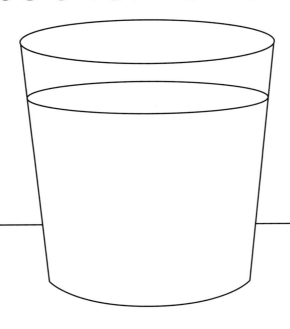

2

I see fireflies.

3

I see watermelon.

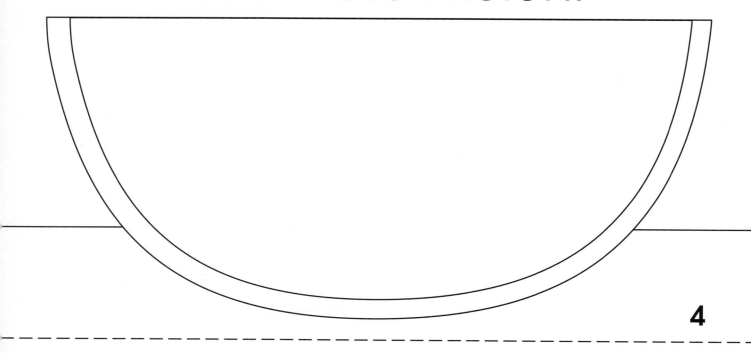

4

I see a swimming pool.

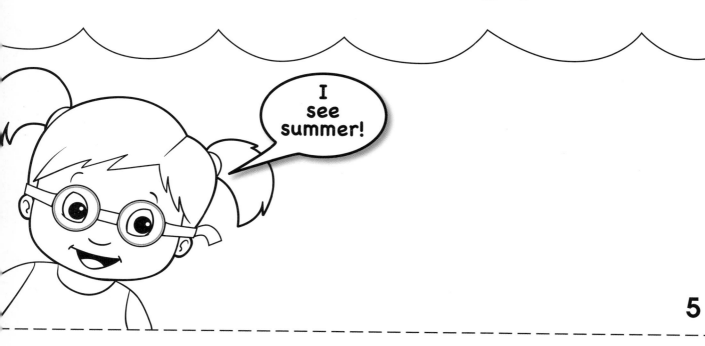

5

Learning Centers

Learning Centers

Bag Bowling
Gross-motor skills, number recognition

Write a numeral from 1 to 10 on each of ten paper lunch bags. Fill each bag with crumpled paper and staple it closed. Arrange the bags like bowling pins and set a small ball nearby. A child rolls the ball toward the bags. Then he names the number on each bag he knocks down.

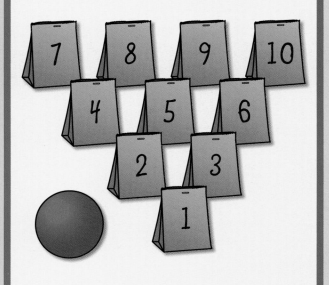

Coarse and Soft
Sensory Center

Materials for one:
coarse sandpaper
soft craft items, such as cotton balls, cotton batting, feathers, and pom-poms
glue

Art process:
1. Feel the coarseness of the sandpaper; then squeeze a generous amount of glue on the sandpaper.
2. Choose a desired material, feel its texture, and then press it on the glue.
3. Repeat Steps 1 and 2 with other materials.

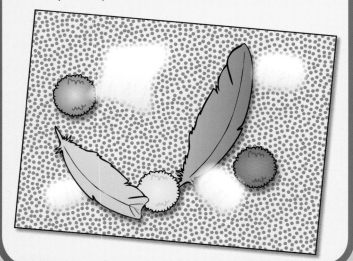

Sandy Writing
Writing Center

Forming letters in the sand helps little ones improve their letter-writing skills. Place a set of letter cards at your sand table along with a small plastic shovel. Lightly dampen the sand. A youngster chooses a letter card and then uses her index finger to form the letter in the sand. When she is satisfied with her work, she erases the letter by dragging the shovel over the sand. She repeats the process with the remaining letter cards as desired.

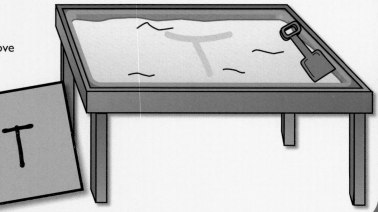

Learning Centers

Heart Designs
Math Center

Here's a simple Valentine's Day–themed patterning activity! Make a supply of red and pink heart cutouts. Then place them at a table along with a blank calendar grid. Prompt students to visit the table and place the hearts on the grid to make a pattern. For more advanced students, provide purple heart cutouts as well! *Patterning*

Janet Boyce
Hinojosa Early Childhood and Pre-Kindergarten Center
Houston, TX

Supersize Soup!
Literacy Center

Soup is the best on a cold winter day! For this center, float craft foam letter cutouts in your water table and provide a big pot, a ladle, bowls, and spoons. Encourage students to identify the letters in this alphabet soup while they take part in soup-themed dramatic play! *Identifying letters*

Christine Angst
St. Paul's Nursery School
Cincinnati, OH

Stunning Craftsmanship
Art Center

Gather a supply of boxes in different shapes and sizes and provide an assortment of collage materials. Encourage each child to explore his creativity by decorating a box using materials of his choice. *Expressing oneself through art*

Learning Centers

Emoticon Lids
Game Center

In advance, gather pairs of identical lids. Then do an Internet search for emoticon images. Choose a desired set of emoticons and make two copies. Then print them, cut them out, and attach each one to a lid. Place the lids facedown at a center. Youngsters take turns flipping two lids, attempting to make a match. If the lids don't match, the child flips them back over. When he finds a match, he names the emotion and then removes the pair of lids from the game. Students continue until all the emoticons have been matched. *Identifying emotions*

Deborah J. Ryan
Newberg, OR

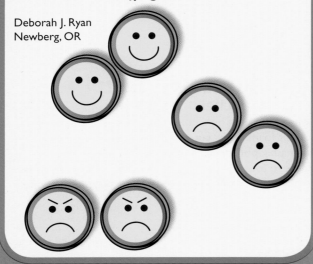

Trace My Face
Fine-Motor Area

Place dry-erase markers near your classroom mirror. A child visits the center and chooses a marker. Then he looks at himself and draws his face on the mirror, adding details as desired. He erases his masterpiece for the next student. *Developing fine-motor skills*

Tricia Kylene Brown, Bowling Green, KY

Finding Food
Science Center

Scatter birdseed in a shallow tub. Then cover the birdseed with water and place the tub in the freezer. When the water is frozen, place the tub at a center along with pairs of tweezers. Encourage little ones to pretend the tweezers are beaks and to use them to try to remove the birdseed. Guide little ones to determine that it might be difficult for birds to find food in the winter. *Investigating living things*

Janet Boyce
Hinojosa Early Childhood and Pre-Kindergarten Center
Houston, TX

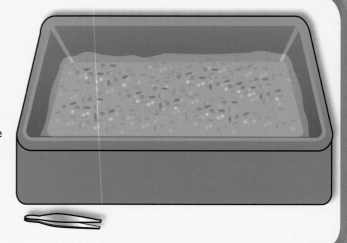

Where Are the Eggs?
Math Center

Make a copy of the front-facing bunny on page 299 for each child. Have a child color and cut out the bunny and glue it to the middle of a sheet of construction paper. Next, say, "Draw an egg above the bunny." Watch to make sure the child is drawing the egg in the correct location. Then continue by giving instructions that involve the positional words *below* and *beside*. Finally, have her color the eggs!
Positional words

Nancy Vogt, Boothbay Head Start, Boothbay, ME

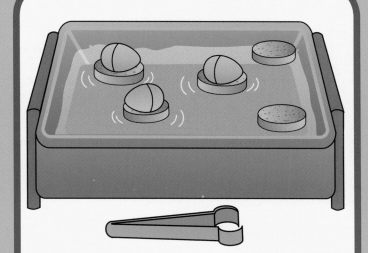

Eggs and Ham Float
Water Table

Spotlight Dr. Seuss's birthday (March 2) at this center! Float sponges (ham slices) in your water table. (Pink ones are particularly fetching because they look more hamlike.) Provide green plastic eggs and tongs. A child visits the center and uses the tongs to attempt to carefully place a green egg on each piece of ham.
Spatial skills, fine-motor skills

Janet Boyce
Hinojosa Early Childhood and Pre-Kindergarten Center
Houston, TX

A Wacky Rainbow
Teacher-guided play

Brighten up your classroom with these unique paintings! Place a rainbow cutout in a lidded plastic container. Help each child dip marbles into colorful paint and then place them on the paper. Next, secure the lid and prompt the child to shake the container. Remove the lid to reveal a wacky and wonderful rainbow! ***Expressing oneself through art***

Learning Centers

Parents and Children
Literacy Center

This uppercase and lowercase matching center is perfect for Mother's Day and Father's Day! Cut out a copy of the people patterns on page 117. Label each mother-daughter pair and father-son pair with matching uppercase and lowercase letters. (Depending on your class, you may want to create only a few pairs.) Then place them at a center. Youngsters match the letters by pairing the family members! *Matching uppercase and lowercase letters*

Cindy Zsittnik
Huntersville, NC

It's a House!
Art Center

Little ones transform envelopes into houses at this center! Place a variety of envelopes of different sizes in your art center along with construction paper scraps. A youngster opens an envelope and places it so the opening is facing down. Then she uses the scraps and crayons to embellish her house, adding any desired details. These houses look adorable displayed in a row! *Expressing oneself through art*

Cindy Hoying
Centerville, OH

Pick a Pint
Fine-Motor Area

Trim a length of green bulletin board paper so it resembles a row of strawberry plants and place the paper on the floor. Then scatter red pom-poms (strawberries) on the paper. Provide small baskets and tongs. Youngsters visit the center and use the tongs to "pick" berries and place them in the baskets. *Developing fine-motor skills*

Marcell Gibison, Ephrata Church of the Brethren Child Center, Ephrata, PA

Tasty Worms!
Sensory Center

This process art is a fun sensory center! Give each child cold cooked spaghetti noodles on a colorful paper plate. Encourage him to touch the noodles, swirl them around, and arrange them as desired. Then have him attach a bird cutout (patterns on page 118) to the edge of the plate. When the noodles dry, they remain attached to the paper plate. Now that bird has a plate full of worms! ***Exploring the sense of touch***

Measurement Inspectors
Math Center

Place a supply of colorful streamers at your math center along with clipboards with paper and writing utensils. Encourage a child to choose a streamer, clipboard, and utensil. Then have him compare the length of the streamer to things in the classroom, making "official notes" on his clipboard. Change up this center by encouraging youngsters to find things that are shorter than the streamer. ***Nonstandard measurement***

What Are They Saying?
Writing Center

Place copies of page 119 at your writing center. Have a child dictate what she thinks the frogs are talking about. Write her words at the bottom of the page. Then have her color the picture. You may also wish to use this center without dictation so children can use invented spelling and scribbles to write about the frogs' conversation. ***Writing***

Picnic Centers

So Many Ants!
Math Center

Get scrapbook paper that resembles picnic tablecloths. Then laminate the paper. Gather a small group of youngsters and give each child a sheet of paper and a small cup with ten raisins (ants). Prompt each child to place five ants on her paper. Then have her eat one. Ask, "How many ants are left?" Next, have children add two ants to the paper. Then have them eat three. Once again, have them report the number of ants left. Continue in the same way until all the ants have been eaten!

Sarah Sant
First Baptist Church
Sulphur Springs, TX

Picnic Preferences
Social Studies Center

A glyph is a fun way for little ones to share information about themselves! Lead small groups of students to color a copy of page 120 to match their responses to the key shown. Then help each child share the information on her paper.

Key

Where do you like to eat?
inside—yellow picnic basket
outside—orange picnic basket

Do you like to eat sandwiches?
yes—brown sandwich
no—green sandwich

Which is your favorite drink?
water—blue cup
juice—purple cup
milk—white cup

What color apple is your favorite?
red apple
green apple
yellow apple

One-of-a-Kind Burgers
Writing Center

A burger is a great option for a picnic! And youngsters will surely enjoy creating their own unique burgers. Give a youngster a copy of page 121. Have him draw unique burger fixings between the buns and then write (or dictate) what is in his burger. These pages are cute bound into a class book!

My burger _has pickles, birthday cake, and pizza on it._

Bear Centers

Find the *B*s!
Literacy Center

Help little ones understand that *bear* begins with the letter *B*! Gather letter cards, including several *B*s. (Depending on your students' letter knowledge, you may want to include lowercase *B*s as well.) Then place them at a center faceup. Provide a supply of bear counters. A child visits the center and places a bear on each *B*! ***Recognizing letters, letter-sound association***

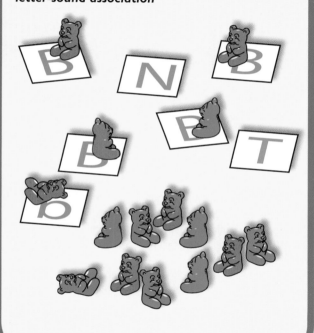

Reading "Bear-y" Quietly
Reading Area

Drape a brown blanket over a table so it resembles a cave. Then place stuffed bear toys in the cave, along with flashlights and bear-themed books. (See the great suggestions given.) Little ones crawl into the cave and use a flashlight to look at the books. ***Developing print and book awareness***

Jamberry by Bruce Degen
We're Going on a Bear Hunt retold by Michael Rosen
Bear Snores On by Karma Wilson
A Visitor for Bear by Bonny Becker
Every Autumn Comes the Bear by Jim Arnosky

Standing Bear
Art Center

To make the bear's body, fold a 9" x 12" sheet of brown construction paper in half. Tear off both corners from the folded edge; then tear a semicircle from both thicknesses of the open edge as shown. Tear a bear head from a 6" circle of brown construction paper and two ears from small brown construction paper scraps. Draw facial features with a black marker, and glue the ears to the head and the head to the folded edge of the paper. Add toes to the two front feet with the black marker. Unfold the paper slightly to make the bear stand on a tabletop. ***Developing fine-motor skills***

Presidents' Day
Centers

Introduce youngsters to this holiday
with some presidential exploration!

Who's That?
Fine-Motor Area

Gather a few students and show them a one-dollar bill and a five-dollar bill. Have youngsters study the currency. Then tell them that the man on the one-dollar bill is George Washington and he was the first president of our country. Next, explain that the man on the five-dollar bill is Abraham Lincoln. He was our 16th president and is known for being a very good and smart man. Next, store the money for safekeeping and then give each child a copy of page 122. Help her identify George Washington and Abraham Lincoln. Then have her follow the directions to complete the page. *Developing fine-motor skills*

The President's Residence
Block Center

Print a photo of the White House. (An Internet image search will turn up plenty of options.) Explain to youngsters that this is where the president lives. Then display the photo near your block center. Students visit the center and use blocks to build a presidential residence using the White House as a reference. *Spatial skills*

Janet Boyce
Hinojosa Early Childhood and Pre-Kindergarten Center
Houston, TX

L or W?
Literacy Center

Place paper pennies and quarters in a bag. Then write the letters *L* and *W* on separate sheets of paper. A child removes a coin and decides which president is on it. If it's Lincoln, she says "/l/, /l/, Lincoln!" and if it's Washington, she says, "/w/, /w/, Washington." Then she places the coin on the corresponding letter. Youngsters continue in the same way, taking turns, until all the coins have been removed from the bag and placed on a letter. *Letter-sound association*

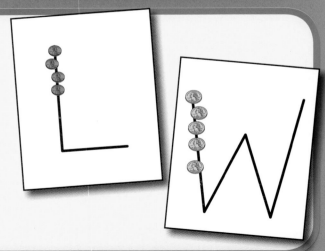

©The Mailbox®

©The Mailbox®

©The Mailbox®

©The Mailbox®

Bird Patterns
Use with "Tasty Worms!" on page 113.

Note to the teacher: Use with "What Are They Saying?" on page 113.

©The Mailbox®

Note to the teacher: Use with "Picnic Preferences" on page 114.

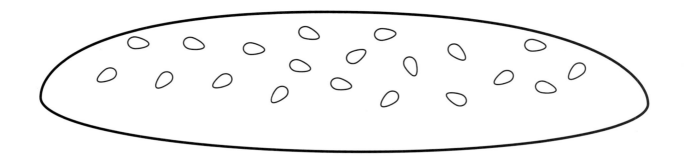

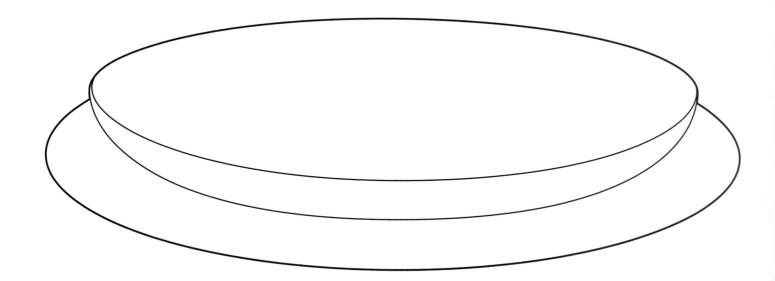

My burger _____

_____

Presidential Party

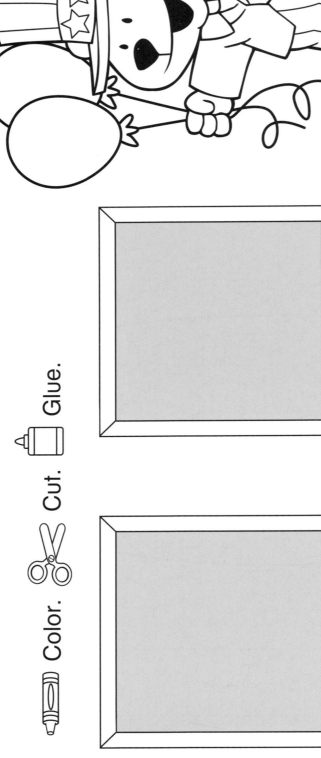

Color. Cut. Glue.

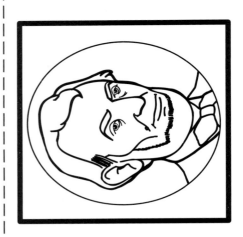

OUR READERS SHARE

Our Readers Share

Project Pictures!
I send home lots of craft projects at the end of the school year and always give parents this bit of advice: Attach all the projects to a wall, have your youngster pose in front of it, and take a photo. Then choose specific projects to keep and recycle the rest. That way you'll have a photo to remember all the fun projects from preschool, but you won't have to store them all! *Karen Thurber, Karen's Day Care, Wisconsin Rapids, WI*

Concept Crowns
I like to have a special week in which children wear concept crowns! At the beginning of the week, my students make and decorate paper crowns. Then, each time a child demonstrates knowledge of a concept—such as identifying a number, a letter, a color, or a shape—I attach a sticky dot to his crown. My little ones love to take their crowns home at the end of the week to show their parents! *Marcell Gibison, Ephrata Church of the Brethren Children's Center, Ephrata, PA*

Vibrant Visors!
To make an extra fun Crazy Hat Day and Beach Day, I went to a local craft store and purchased inexpensive craft foam visors and foam stickers. My students had a great time decorating the visors and wearing them for both of the special days! *Ashley Lutts, St. Albans Childcare Center, Louisville, KY*

Kindergarten Readiness Night
Some of my students are fearful about what kindergarten will be like when they come back to school in the fall. To alleviate these fears, I have a kindergarten readiness night! I invite last year's preschoolers who are now in kindergarten and their families as well as the current preschoolers who will be entering kindergarten. The kindergartners share stories about their class. We have pizza, and the children get to play at the classroom centers. I've received lots of compliments on this fun evening! *Suzanne Foote, East Ithaca Preschool, Ithaca, NY*

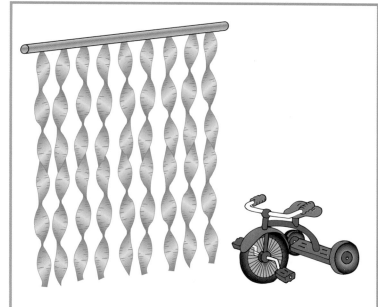

Through the Car Wash!

My little ones love it when I bring my car wash prop outside during outdoor play! To make a car wash prop, I attach blue streamers to a dowel. Then, when my students ride tricycles, I hold the dowel over their roadway so they can drive the tricycles through the streamers. What a fun car wash! *Keely Hallin, Bonney Lake Early Childhood Education and Assistance Program, Bonney Lake, WA*

Book-Themed Decor

When I get new hardcover books in my classroom, I remove the paper book covers from the books. (They always get torn up anyway!) Then I use them as wall decorations in my classroom. My little ones love to look at the book covers on the wall! *Mary Richardson, Foundations Early Learning Center, Cape Coral, FL*

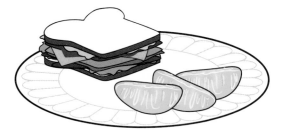

Table Manners

My preschool class eats lunch family-style in our room. To encourage table manners, I ask the children to wait until all their friends are seated before they begin eating. Once everyone is in his seat, I lead students in reciting the rhyme shown. Then we have our lunch! *Kathy Young, Beale Elementary, Gallipolis Ferry, WV*

Eye-Catching Posters!

To make classroom and hallway signs more attractive, I attach bulletin board border around the edges and then laminate them for durability. The resulting signs are more fun to look at and catch the eye of both students and parents. *Carole L. Watkins, Timothy Ball Elementary, Crown Point, IN*

Our Readers Share

Open House Scavenger Hunt

I use the story *If You Give a Mouse a Cookie* by Laura Numeroff as the theme for my welcome-to-school open house! I give each family a folder with a mouse on it and a list of instructions inside, like those shown. The family members and their preschooler go through the instructions and get to know the classroom. Then they have a real treat of cookies and milk when they are finished! *Robin Deaton, Washington County YMCA Preschool, Salem, IN*

Check out page 131 for mouse, cookie, and milk patterns!

Welcome!

1. Mr. Mouse loves cookies. Please find one cookie at one of our tables and sit down to color it. Place the colorful cookie in your folder.

2. Now that he has a cookie, he would really like a glass of milk to go with it. Locate the drinking fountain in the classroom. Find the glass of milk with your name on it, remove it from the wall, and place it in your folder.

3. Now that he has had a cookie and milk, he will probably need a napkin. Ms. Norris, our classroom assistant, is giving out napkins near the block center. Say hello to Ms. Norris, take a napkin, and place it in your folder.

Return to school on your first day and Ms. Deaton will finish the story about this hungry little mouse! Please stop by the snack table for your own cookies and milk. Feel free to explore more of the classroom before picking up a preschool packet near the exit door!

Bumpy Gourd Monsters!

My little ones love to make monster faces with unique and bumpy gourds! I place the gourds at my art center along with craft glue, paper scraps, large googly eyes, and other supplies. When a child visits the center, he chooses a gourd and transforms it into a monster face as desired. The gourds always turn out very fun and unique! *Melissa Carroll, Southmont Elementary, Asheboro, NC*

Candy Corn Bags

To make these cute treat bags, I show my youngsters a piece of candy corn and we discuss the order of the three colors on the piece of candy. Then I have each student paint a paper bag so it looks like a piece of candy corn. After I fill each bag with a few fall treats, I tie it closed with a piece of raffia. *Bonnie Martin, Ewing, NJ*

Friendship Turkeys

To make friendship turkeys, I ask my students how many hands they have. After each child determines that he has two, I ask how many people we need to have four hands. I help them conclude that two people would have four hands. Next, I help two youngsters make colorful handprints in a fan shape on a sheet of paper. Then I have them glue eyes, a beak, and a wattle to a construction paper turkey body (see pattern below). They then glue the body in front of the handprints. We love our cooperative turkey project! *Ann Miller, Ann's Bright Beginnings Preschool, Paulding, OH*

Holiday Magnets

These simple magnets make great holiday gifts! I cut a photo of a child to fit inside a rectangular lid from a baby food container. Then I help the child glue his photo inside the lid. Next, I help him glue decorative trim around the edge and magnetic tape to the back of the lid. *Sharon Newman, St. Matthew's Child Care Center, St. Louis, MO*

Turkey Body Pattern

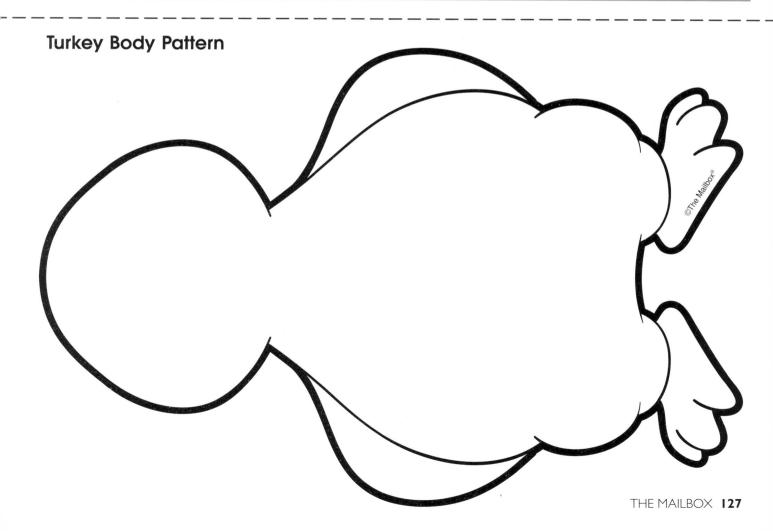

©The Mailbox®

Our Readers Share

Add a Link!

For a fun behavior management system, I use tape to attach a plastic link manipulative to a wall beneath each child's name card. Then each day, when the child completes his class job, I have him add a link. I also have a child add a link whenever I catch him doing something nice. When the chain of links touches the floor, the child gets to choose a special item from our treasure chest. My little ones love this system! *Jenna Kasik, Aero Special Education Cooperative, Burbank, IL*

Sweet Treat Can

These Valentine's Day gifts always turn out super sweet! To make one, I collect a small container with a lid for each child. Over a few days, I take photos of each child. Then I have each student press his photos facedown on a strip of Con-Tact covering sized to fit around the container. I help him attach the strip to the container. We fill the container with Valentine's Day candies and cookies, and I attach a cute poem tag (see page 132) that the student has signed to the lid. *Pauline Rodriquez, Little People's Preschool, Union City, CA*

So Colorful!

On snowy days, I add food coloring and water to empty dish soap bottles. Then I take youngsters outside and allow them to use the bottles to decorate the snow with lines and designs. My students love this unique outdoor activity, and it's terrific for fine- and gross-motor skills! *Joanne Kautz, Holy Trinity Tiny Trojans Preschool, Winsted, MN*

A Winter Picnic!

Having a winter picnic in the classroom is so much fun. I put white sheets on the floor and encourage students to wear scarves and hats. Then we sit on the sheets and partake of white treats, such as yogurt-covered pretzels and vanilla yogurt. It's such a fun experience! *Jerilyn Stebbins, Tiny Treasures Nursery School, Kenhorst, PA*

Our Readers Share

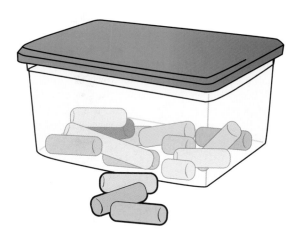

Chalkboard Fun!

To make a neat chalkboard center in my room, I attach Con-Tact Chalkboard Liner paper to a side of my desk. I provide a container full of colored chalk and a chalkboard eraser. Then I invite a small number of youngsters to visit the center to draw on this unique chalkboard. I've also found that playing with the chalkboard works well as a special privilege that needs to be earned. *Janet Schwan, Fairport, NY*

Grab a Clipboard

My youngsters frequently need paper in their centers to make signs, "write" pretend restaurant orders, or draw pictures. To give them easy access to paper, I've stocked several clipboards with paper and attached pencils, and I store them in an inexpensive letter divider from an office supply store. This way when my youngsters need paper, they can just walk over and grab a clipboard! *Diane Johnson, Steps to Success Preschool, Willoughby, OH*

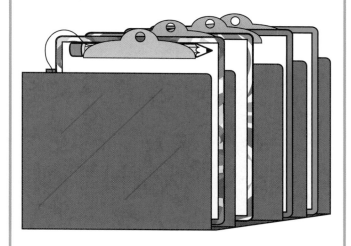

Our Favorites

The Best of the Month!

I love to have my little ones work on their recall skills. At the end of each day, I have students recall the highlights of that day. I write their thoughts on a sheet of chart paper. Near the end of the month, I use these notes to have students vote for their favorite songs, snacks, games, and other activities. Then the final day of the month is filled with all our favorites. My students love this! *Carole Watkins, Timothy Ball Elementary, Crown Point, IN*

"Smellies"!

I enjoy providing different incentives for my youngsters as a classroom management tool. Instead of using stickers or stamps, I purchase several lip balm sticks in a variety of scents. When a child answers a question correctly or makes a good choice, I give him a "smelly" by rubbing a bit of the lip balm on the back of his hand. My students love to smell their "smellies," and I love this simple and inexpensive tool! *Cristina Calvario, Perales Elementary, San Antonio, TX*

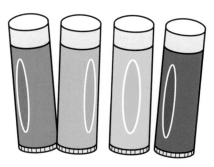

Our Readers Share

A Better Class Book

To make class books that last, I put page protectors in a binder that has a see-through window in the front. Then I simply slip each child's page in a page protector and put a cover for the book in the front window. These books hold up really well in my reading area! *Erica Holland, Quality Child Care, Fort Smith, AR*

Wrapping Paper Shakers

I don't throw away sheets of wrapping paper used for birthday presents or holidays; I reuse them to make music shakers! I cut wrapping paper into strips and stack a few strips. Then I fold the strips in half and staple them in place near the fold. Next, I use heavy-duty tape to attach the folded strips to a craft stick. My kids love to hold the craft stick and shake the prop when we sing songs. *Sharon Boullion, Crowley, LA*

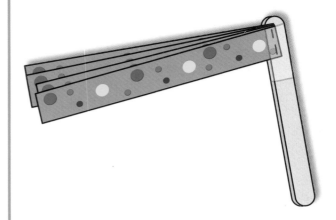

Take-Home Clay

My students love this summertime present! Near the end of the school year, I whip up my favorite recipe of play dough and place some in a container for each child. I cut a white paper circle to fit each lid and label the lids as shown. This gift always makes a big impression! *Lucia Kemp Henry, Fallon, NV*

A Father's Day Thank-You!

Families come in many shapes and sizes, so I like to have my students make a Father's Day gift that can go to any adult who helps and cares for them. I simply have each child make colorful handprints on a sheet of paper. Then, beneath the prints, I write the text shown. This project is always appreciated by everyone! *Loucinda Copley, Daniels Elementary, Daniels, WV*

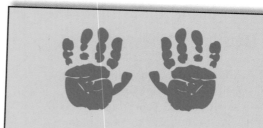

For the big hands that take care of my little hands—Thank You!

©The Mailbox®

©The Mailbox®

©The Mailbox®

Heart Tags

Use with "Sweet Treat Can" on page 128.

When I am at school and we're far apart,
You might get sad, but you're in my heart.
Here are some sweets for when I'm away.
I love you so much! Happy Valentine's Day.

©The Mailbox®

When I am at school and we're far apart,
You might get sad, but you're in my heart.
Here are some sweets for when I'm away.
I love you so much! Happy Valentine's Day.

©The Mailbox®

When I am at school and we're far apart,
You might get sad, but you're in my heart.
Here are some sweets for when I'm away.
I love you so much! Happy Valentine's Day.

©The Mailbox®

When I am at school and we're far apart,
You might get sad, but you're in my heart.
Here are some sweets for when I'm away.
I love you so much! Happy Valentine's Day.

©The Mailbox®

PROBLEM SOLVED!

Problem Solved!

How do you help *shy students?*

Your Solutions to Classroom Challenges

To help shy students, write a "**thought question**" on your board and read it aloud to youngsters. Then, at the end of the day, ask each child to share an answer to the question. Repeated sharing and encouragement helps shy youngsters become more comfortable in the classroom.

> What is your favorite toy to play with at home?

I help a shy child by **sitting and playing** with him in one of our centers. I begin by asking the child to complete tasks, such as making the baby a bottle in the housekeeping center or stacking the tall blocks in the block center. Other youngsters will naturally gravitate toward our play. Then I can encourage the shy youngster to complete tasks with a classmate, such as helping the other child find a baby blanket. Pretty soon, I'm not needed and the child is playing happily.

Darlene Butler Taig, Willow Creek Cooperative Preschool, Westland, MI

> Play on the slide.
> Pretend to be mommies.
> Watch a movie.
> Eat pizza.
> Play with the trucks.
> Swing.
> Squeeze the play dough.
> Ride the tricycles.
> Paint.

It helps to give a shy child ideas about **what friends can do together**. I have my little ones share ideas and I write them down on a sheet of chart paper. It's amazing the ideas that youngsters can come up with!

Bonnie Krum, St. Matthew's Early Education Center, Bowie, MD

For extra fun, give a child a copy of page 139 and have her write her name. Then have her dictate her favorite thing to do with a friend. Write her words and prompt her to add a drawing. Then bind the pages together to make a class book.

likes to __play on the swings__ with a friend.

It's your turn!
themailbox.com/magazine/submit-idea

How do you organize and display *classroom jobs?*

Your Solutions to Classroom Challenges

Try choosing just one helper who does all the jobs for the day! Cut a piece of blue construction paper so it resembles a pond. Then personalize a duck cutout for each child and laminate the ducks. (See page 140 for a duck pattern.)

Attach your little ones' ducks to the pond. Then tape a yellow craft feather to the tail feathers of the duck with the name of your daily helper.

Short on space? Combine your job display with a birthday display! Write each child's name and birthdate on a cupcake cutout. (See page 140 for a cupcake pattern.) Make construction paper hat cutouts and label each one with a different job. Then simply attach each hat to a different cupcake. Each week, move the hats to reassign jobs.

Try using a sign-in sheet! Write each job title on the left side of a large sheet of paper. Then add a blank next to each job and laminate the paper. Choose a child for each job and have her sign in with a wipe-off marker. Display the chart and, after a week, erase the names and have different youngsters sign the paper.

Kelly Lynaugh, Fair Garden Preschool, Knoxville, TN

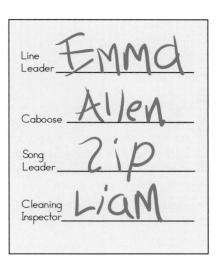

It's your turn!
themailbox.com/magazine/submit-idea

Your Solutions to Classroom Challenges

I have each child stand by his circle time seat. Then I begin **counting backward** slowly from five to zero. During that time, students pick up as many scraps as they can without talking or running. My students have a lot of fun with this cleanup game!

Susan Bunyan, Linn Elementary, Dodge City, KS

5 . . . 4 . . . 3 . . . 2 . . .

Singing is a great way to get my little ones motivated to clean the classroom. This is one of their favorite songs!

(sung to the tune of "If You're Happy and You Know It")

If the room is looking messy, clean it up! (Clap, clap!)
If the room is looking messy, clean it up! (Clap, clap!)
On the tables, on the floor, clean it up and find some more.
If the room is looking messy, clean it up! (Clap, clap!)

Kate Hogenson, Preschools of St. Andrew's, Mahtomedi, MN

To help my preschoolers stay focused on cleaning up, I make **necklaces** with index cards and yarn. Each necklace shows the name and picture of a group of items that need to be cleaned up, such as blocks, toy cars, or play food. Each child chooses a necklace to wear and begins cleaning. If a child forgets his cleanup focus, he just takes a look at his necklace!

Sherry Price, Kid Connections Child Care, Park Rapids, MN

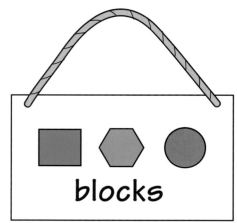

blocks

Check out page 141 for **cleanup awards**!

It's your turn!
themailbox.com/magazine/submit-idea

How do you encourage youngsters to *clean up the classroom?*

What do you do when you have *time to fill* before the next activity?

Your Solutions to Classroom Challenges

 I have a cute basket decorated with ribbons. Every time we learn a new song, I place a corresponding **song card** in this basket. Then, when there's some time to fill before the next activity, I have a child choose a song card and we sing the song. I always make sure there are a variety of holiday songs in the basket, because little ones get such a kick out of singing them at odd times throughout the year!

Sue Reppert, Widening World Preschool, Mentor, OH

 To fill time between activities, I have a **fun box**! In the box, I've placed slips of paper with various simple activities. My students know that I will choose a child who is sitting quietly to pick a slip of paper. Then we complete the activity. I continue until it's time for us to move on.

Sara Irwin, Peace Lutheran Preschool Flagstaff, AZ

To make your own **FUN BOX**, cut out a copy of the cards on page 142 and place them in a decorated box. Then use them as described.

 Waiting cards are my time-filler secret! I laminate a variety of card sets, such as numbers, shapes, nursery rhymes, land animals, ocean animals, bugs, and birds. Then I bind the cards with metal rings. After we have bathroom time and students wash their hands, they get to pick a set of waiting cards to look through. This keeps them occupied until everyone is ready for the next activity.

Melissa Bates, Kewanee Pre-K Lyle School, Kewanee, IL

It's your turn!
themailbox.com/magazine/submit-idea

Problem Solved!

How do you encourage parents to *read aloud to their little ones?*

Your Solutions to Classroom Challenges

 I invite a different parent to the classroom to **read aloud each week**. I encourage the parent to choose the book with her child and to practice reading it aloud before her designated storytime date. Then I make a video recording of the event and email it to the parent. The joy of reading aloud always encourages more "performances" at home!

Jami Bernier Whitley, Dacula, GA

 To encourage reading aloud, I put a pack of blank drawing paper and a storybook in a **take-home literacy pack**. The parent and child read the book and then work together to draw a scene from the story. When the pack comes back, I display the artwork and then give the pack to a different child to take home.

Tina Benson, Providence Elementary, Scottsboro, AL

I do a "**Reading Caterpillar**" with my students. I send home circle cutouts, and each time a parent reads a book aloud, he writes the name of the book on a circle. He sends the circle back to school with his child, and I attach it to the wall next to a circle decorated like a caterpillar head. This caterpillar ends up crawling all over the room!

Amber Knies, Krazy About Kidz, Jasper, IN

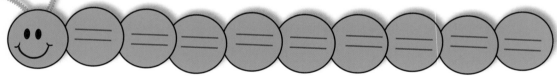

 A "**Borrowing Box**" helps encourage my parents! They can choose a book from our classroom borrowing box to take home and read to their child. Then they can return the book and take a new one!

Nicole DeVincenzo, Rankin I Head Start NC Pre-K Program, Gastonia, NC

 I beg the parents! Seriously. I emphasize that reading is the skill that will unlock all other skill areas. I also send home suggestions on questions to ask when they read to their child and **research** that states the importance of reading aloud.

Alicia Kirkham Cate, Lorene Smith Kirkpatrick Elementary, Maypearl, TX

It's your turn!
themailbox.com/magazine/submit-idea

_____ likes to _____

with a friend.

Note to the teacher: Use with page 134.

Duck Pattern
Use with the first idea on page 135.

©The Mailbox®

Cupcake Pattern
Use with the second idea on page 135.

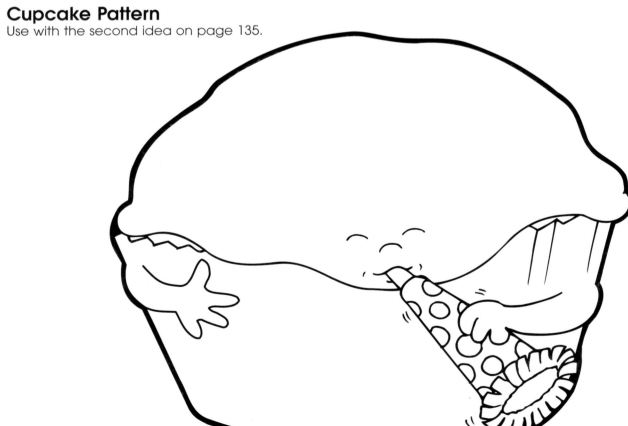

©The Mailbox®

_____

name

did a "bear-y" good job during cleanup time!

_____

teacher

_____

date

©The Mailbox®

_____

name

did a "bear-y" good job during cleanup time!

_____

teacher

_____

date

©The Mailbox®

Fun Box Cards

Use with the second idea on page 137.

Say the alphabet while marching around the room.

©The Mailbox®

Sing "Head and Shoulders."

©The Mailbox®

Shake hands with your neighbor.

©The Mailbox®

Count to 30 while patting your knees.

©The Mailbox®

Play animal charades.

©The Mailbox®

Sing "Bingo."

©The Mailbox®

Count all the legs in the room.

©The Mailbox®

Count to 20 using monster voices and mouse voices.

©The Mailbox®

Clap the syllables in student names.

©The Mailbox®

Choose two students and name how they are alike and different.

©The Mailbox®

Dance to music.

©The Mailbox®

Move like the following animals: snakes, frogs, elephants, and owls.

©The Mailbox®

Songs & Such

Songs & Such

To the Beach!

(sung to the tune of "If You're Happy and You Know It")

If you're going to the beach, what should you wear?
If you're going to the beach, what should you wear?
It's important that you wear [sunglasses] while you're there.   *Curl finger and thumb around eyes.*
If you're going to the beach, what should you wear?

Continue with the following: a sun hat *(touch head)*, sunscreen *(rub arm)*, flip-flops *(alternate lifting flattened hands)*

Camping Is Fun!

Here is a chant that spotlights fun camping activities!

Here is the tent	*Tent fingers.*
Beneath the trees,	*Sway arms above head.*
Under the shining sun.	*Circle arms above head.*
I'll fish for lunch and eat outside.	*Pretend to reel in a fish.*
Camping is so much fun!	*Clap to the rhythm.*
Here is the tent	*Sway arms above head.*
Beside the fire,	*Flutter fingers.*
Under the shining moon.	*Circle arms above head.*
I'll sing and eat s'mores and sleep.	*Sway.*
Tomorrow will be here soon.	*Lay cheek against folded hands.*

Happy Birthday, USA!

Have little ones wave small American flags as they sing this song!

(sung to the tune of "Yankee Doodle")

March in a parade today
And hold our flag up high.
Watch its colors gently wave
On the Fourth of July!

Happy birthday, USA!
It's our special day.
We celebrate our country's birth
On Independence Day!

Good Morning!

(sung to the tune of "The Farmer in the Dell")

Good morning to the sky.   *Hold arms overhead.*
Good morning to the sun.   *Curve arms overhead.*
Good morning to my family.   *Gesture outward with arms.*
I'm ready for some fun.   *Point to self.*

Good morning to my school   *Point around the room.*
And to all of my friends.   *Wave at friends.*
Good morning to my teacher too.   *Wave at teacher.*
I'm ready to begin!

Songs & Such

Clean Up!

Lead students in singing this song when center time has come to an end!

(sung to the tune of "Row, Row, Row Your Boat")

Clean, clean, clean the room;
Put your things away.
Make the room so nice and neat
For another day!

Clothing Colors

Seat youngsters in a circle. Then lead them in singing the song shown, prompting students wearing green to stand up. When the song is finished, have the students sit down. Then repeat the song, replacing *green* with a different color.

(sung to the tune of "If You're Happy and You Know It")

If you're wearing something [green], please stand up.
If you're wearing something [green], please stand up.
Stand right up! Say, "Look at me!"
There is [green], you'll plainly see!
If you're wearing something [green], please stand up!

Amy King
Pioneer Trail Dayschool
New Smyrna Beach, FL

It's Getting Cooler!

It's almost fall! Celebrate sweater weather with this action rhyme.

Cooler weather—	*Hug self and shiver.*
Wear a sweater.	*Run hands down arms.*
Leaves turn red and brown.	*Hold arms overhead.*
Windy breezes	*Sweep arms back and forth.*
In the "tree-zes."	*Continue sweeping.*
Leaves fall to the ground!	*Flutter fingers down to the floor.*

Raking Leaves

(sung to the tune of "My Bonnie Lies Over the Ocean")

I raked all the leaves in the morning.	*Pretend to rake.*
I raked them all into a mound.	*Rake.*
But then the fall winds came a-blowing.	*Move arms to represent wind.*
The leaves blew back over the ground!	*Wiggle fingers horizontally.*
Raking, raking!	*Pretend to rake.*
The leaves blow back over the ground, the ground!	*Wiggle fingers horizontally.*
Raking, raking! The leaves blow back over the ground!	*Pretend to rake; wiggle fingers horizontally.*

Songs & Such

Five Orange Pumpkins

Make five pumpkin cutouts and attach them to your board. (See the pattern on page 161.) Lead students in reciting the chant shown, having students remove each pumpkin when indicated.

Five orange pumpkins, sitting by my door.
I cooked a pumpkin pie, and then there were four.
Four orange pumpkins, waiting happily.
I cooked some pumpkin bread, and then there were three.
Three orange pumpkins, waiting just for you.
I cooked some pumpkin stew, and then there were two.
Two orange pumpkins, sitting in the sun.
I made a pumpkin smoothie, and then there was one.
One orange pumpkin—there are no more.
It's now a jack-o'-lantern sitting by the door.

Jack-o'-Lantern Faces

Jack-o'-lanterns grin.	Grin.
Jack-o'-lanterns frown.	Frown.
Jack-o'-lantern faces all over town.	Make a face.
Jack-o'-lanterns happy.	Smile.
Jack-o'-lanterns mean.	Make a mean face.
Jack-o'-lanterns all say, "Happy Halloween!"	Throw arms in the air.

That's How I Help

Invite students to brainstorm chores they can do at home to help their families. Then lead students in this sing-along!

(sung to the tune of "Bingo")

When I am home, I do my chores
So I can help my family!
I can [sweep the floor].
I can [sweep the floor].
I can [sweep the floor].
That's how I help my family!

Continue with the following: *rake the leaves, walk the dog, feed the cat, clean my room, make my bed*

Tom Turkey

Little ones learn about turkeys with this little action chant!

Here is Tom Turkey's beard.*	*Stroke chest.*
Here are Tom Turkey's wings.	*Flap arms.*
Here are Tom Turkey's tail feathers.	*Wiggle fingers so they look like tail feathers.*
He struts around like he's a king.	*Walk proudly.*
Here is Tom Turkey's wattle.	*Wiggle fingers under chin.*
Here is Tom Turkey's beak.	*Move hand like a beak.*
"Gobble, gobble, gobble, gobble!"	*Gobble and strut.*
Is how he sounds when he speaks.	

*A turkey's beard is a cluster of long hairlike feathers that grows from its chest.

Songs & Such

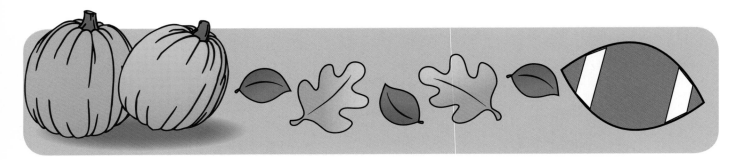

I Am Thankful

Spotlight wonderful things to be thankful for with this action rhyme!

What am I thankful for?   *Shrug.*
Let me see…   *Cock head with hand tapping chin.*
The sun in the sky,   *Put arms above head making a circle.*
The autumn trees,   *Put arms above head, swaying.*
The cooler weather,   *Hug self.*
The falling leaves,   *Wiggle fingers to the floor.*
Thanksgiving dinner,   *Rub stomach.*
Even green peas!   *Shake finger.*
My family, my teacher, and my good friends too,   *Point to teacher and around the room.*
Like you and you and you and you!   *Point to four friends.*

Snowman Melt

This fun action rhyme is perfect for a sunny, yet snowy day!

(sung to the tune of "Twinkle, Twinkle, Little Star")

Sunshine, sunshine, go away;   *Hold arms rounded above head.*
Come to shine another day.   *Shake finger.*
If I see a single ray,   *Shade eyes with hand.*
My snowman will melt away.   *Droop.*
Sunshine, sunshine, go away;   *Hold arms rounded above head.*
Come to shine another day.   *Shake finger.*

Little Stockings

Here's a festive song that encourages counting skills.

(sung to the tune of "Ten Little Indians")

One little, two little, three little stockings;
Four little, five little, six little stockings;
Seven little, eight little, nine little stockings
Hanging on Christmas Eve.

Santa puts goodies in the stockings.
Santa puts goodies in the stockings.
Santa puts goodies in the stockings
Hanging on Christmas Eve.

See page 162 for a **stocking pattern** to use with this song!

Seven Kwanzaa Nights

How many candles are in a kinara? Youngsters learn with this song!

(sung to the tune of "Good Night, Ladies")

Light the candles,
Seven candles.
Light the candles
For seven Kwanzaa nights.

Three red candles,
Three green candles,
One black candle
For seven Kwanzaa nights.

Winter Is...

Give each child a sheet of white paper from your recycle bin. Have her crumple it so it resembles a snowball and place it at her feet. Next, lead students in the action chant shown, prompting them to toss their snowballs when indicated. What fun!

The air is cold.	*Hug self and shiver.*
Snowflakes whirl.	*Wiggle fingers and sway arms.*
Skiers glide.	*Assume a skiing stance and sway.*
Ice-skaters twirl.	*Twirl in a circle.*
Shorter days,	*Hold hands close together.*
Longer nights,	*Hold hands far apart.*
Uh-oh, watch out!	*Hands on cheeks.*
Snowball fights!	*Toss snowball.*

Sledding Fun!

This short and sweet action rhyme is so much fun!

I climb up the snowy hill,	*Pretend to climb.*
Sit down on my sled, and grin.	*Sit and smile.*
Then whoosh!	*Swoop hand downward.*
Gliding down, I go.	
Hop up and do it again!	*Jump up.*

Snowman Melt

Youngsters banish the sunshine with this action song.

(sung to the tune of "Twinkle, Twinkle, Little Star")

Sunshine, sunshine, go away;	*Hold arms rounded above head.*
Come to shine another day.	*Shake finger.*
If I see a single ray,	*Shade eyes with hand.*
My snowman will melt away.	*Droop.*
Sunshine, sunshine, go away;	*Hold arms rounded above head.*
Come to shine another day.	*Shake finger.*

Happy New Year!

Little ones get practice counting backward from ten with this engaging chant!

Watch the clock.	*Slowly sink to the floor in a crouch.*
Get ready to cheer.	
A brand-new year will soon be here.	
Ten, nine, eight, seven, six,	
Five, four, three, two, one—	
Happy New Year!	*Jump up.*

What Will He Do?

Here's a song that reviews the rules of Groundhog Day!

(sung to the tune of "Up on the Housetop")

What will the groundhog do today?
Will he sleep,
Or will he play?
If he sees his shadow
When he peeks,
Winter will be here six more weeks!
Groundhog Day,
Hip hip hooray!
Groundhog Day,
Hip hip hooray!
If there is no shadow, he'll stay out.
Spring will come soon,
There is no doubt!

Won't You Be Mine?

In advance, make a large heart cutout (pattern on page 163). Then lead youngsters in singing the song. At the end, give the heart to a child. Encourage the child to follow you around the room as you sing the song again. Then prompt the child to give the heart to a classmate. Have the two children follow you for another round. Continue until all the youngsters are following you!

(sung to the tune of "This Old Man")

Valentine, valentine,
Won't you be my valentine?
I will always be yours. Won't you be mine too?
Here's my valentine for you!

Ready for Bed

Youngsters will love pretending to be leprechauns with this action chant.

This little leprechaun is ready for bed.	*Point to self.*
He takes his tall hat off his head.	*Pretend to remove hat.*
He wraps himself up, snug and tight,	*Wrap arms around self.*
And falls asleep—good night, good night.	*Close eyes.*
The sun comes up, and he hops out of bed.	*Open eyes and hop.*
He puts his hat back on his head.	*Pretend to put on hat.*
He needs to count his gold today.	*Raise fingers as if counting.*
Then he dances a jig and goes on his way.	*Dance a jig.*

Kite Dancing!

Have little ones use a kite puppet as a prop for this action song! To make one, have each child color and cut out a copy of the kite pattern on page 164. Then have her attach a crepe paper streamer tail.

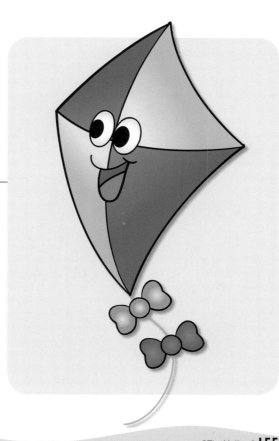

(sung to the tune of "Mary Had a Little Lamb")

Watch my kite dance in the sky.	*Slowly raise kite.*
There it goes. There it flies,	
Swirling left and swirling right.	*Swoop kite to the left and right.*
Dance, my little kite.	*Move kite all around.*
Watch my kite soar in the breeze	*Swoop kite around.*
Over roofs, over trees,	*Swoop kite above head.*
Round and round and up and down.	*Move kite in circles and up and down.*
Land it on the ground.	*Land kite.*

Songs&Such

A Rainy Day

What should students do on a rainy day? They should sing this action song!

(sung to the tune of "London Bridge")

Gentle rain is falling down
Everywhere, all around.
Splitter splat, it's coming down.
Rainy day!

Wiggle fingers from high to low.
Spread arms wide.
Wiggle fingers from high to low.

Grab my raincoat and my hat.
Put on boots, just like that.
Puddles call me out to play.
Rainy day!

Pretend to hold lapels; then touch head.
Pretend to pull on boots.
Stomp.

Earth Day

Sing this song with your little ones when it's time to clean up. Your classroom will be clean in no time, and the song will reinforce keeping the earth clean and neat!

(sung to the tune of "Clementine")

Time to clean up, time to clean up,
Time to throw our trash away.
Put the trash where it belongs.
We make Earth Day every day.

So Many Feelings

Help students recognize feelings with this song!

(sung to the tune of "My Bonnie Lies Over the Ocean")

When I stomp my feet, I am angry.   *Stomp.*
When I cry, I feel very sad.   *Twist fists near eyes.*
When I shake and shiver, I'm scared.   *Hold self and shiver.*
When I smile, I'm happy and glad.   *Trace smile with fingers.*
Feelings, feelings—   *Sway.*
Oh so many feelings you see, you see!   *Continue swaying.*
Feelings, feelings—   *Continue swaying.*
I have lots of feelings in me!   *Continue swaying; point to self.*

Cover Your Mouth

Model the way you would like little ones to cover their mouths when they cough or sneeze after singing this catchy song!

*(sung to the tune of
"Twinkle, Twinkle, Little Star")*

When you cough or when you sneeze,
Cover your mouth, if you please.
That's the healthy thing to do.
Stopping germs is up to you.
When you cough or when you sneeze,
Cover your mouth, if you please.

Making Tunnels

Lead youngsters in singing the song. As they sing, prompt students to press their palms together and then move their hands back and forth to pantomime a wiggling worm!

(sung to the tune of "Yankee Doodle")

Worms make tunnels through the ground
To let in air and rain.
That helps all the roots to grow
And lets the water drain.
Worms can wiggle. Worms can squirm,
Wiggling to and fro,
Making soil healthier—
Go, wiggle worms, go!

Mister Turtle

This cute pond-themed song has adorable actions your youngsters will want to repeat again and again!

(sung to the tune of "Sing a Song of Sixpence")

Here is Mister Turtle
Living in his shell.
His shell protects his insides
and keeps him safe and well.
When he senses danger,
His head and feet pull in.
And when he knows it's safe outside,
He sticks them out again!

Make a fist with thumb out.
Cover fist with a cupped hand.
Wiggle Mister Turtle.

Keep Mister Turtle still.
Hide thumb in fist.

Stick out thumb.

Happy Mother's Day!

Celebrate Mother's Day with this sweet chant!

I'll pick a lot of flowers
And make a big bouquet.
I'll give them to her with a hug.
Happy Mother's Day!

Make picking motions.
Circle arms in front of body.
Hug self.
Draw a heart in the air.

From Wigglers to Listeners

Encourage little ones to wiggle during the first verse and sit quietly during the second!

(sung to the tune of "Ten Little Indians")

One little, two little, three children wiggling,
Four little, five little, six children wiggling,
Seven little, eight little, nine children wiggling.
Let's get those wiggles out!

One little, two little, three children listening,
Four little, five little, six children listening,
Seven little, eight little, nine children listening.
We're ready for circle time!

Kathryn Wilson
New Hope Elementary
Henderson, NC

The Sun Is Out!

Lead little ones in performing this short summer song. After youngsters have performed it several times, consider adding accompaniment with sun shakers! (To make a sun shaker, place uncooked rice or beans between two yellow paper plates and then tape the plates in place.)

(sung to the tune of "The Farmer in the Dell")

The sun is out today—	*Hold arms above head.*
Another summer day.	*Fan self.*
Before it gets too hot for me,	*Wipe brow.*
I run outside to play!	*Run in place.*

Summertime

Spotlight the good and bad of summer with this cool chant!

Summertime sunglasses,	*Circle fingers around eyes.*
Summertime hat,	*Touch head.*
Summertime sunscreen	*Rub arm.*
And ball and bat.	*Pretend to swing a bat.*
Summertime swimming	*Pretend to swim.*
And summertime plants,	*Move arms to mimic a growing plant.*
Summertime sun	*Circle arms above head.*
And summertime ants!	*Wiggle fingers along arm.*

Pumpkin Pattern
Use with "Five Orange Pumpkins" on page 148.

Stocking Patterns
Use with "Little Stockings" on page 151.

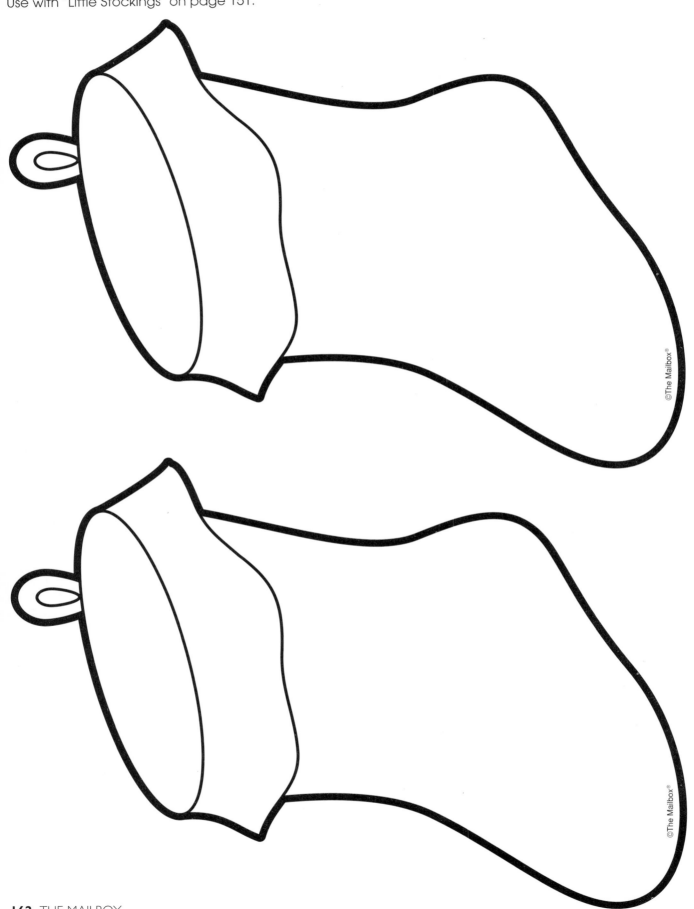

©The Mailbox®

©The Mailbox®

©The Mailbox®

Kite Pattern
Use with "Kite Dancing!" on page 155.

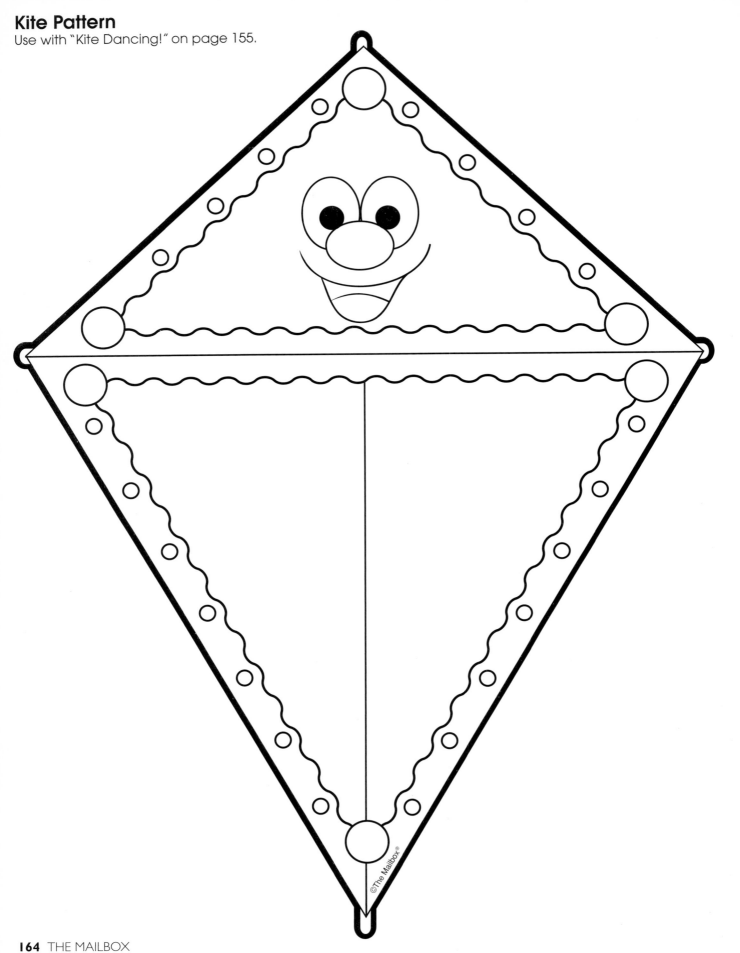

©The Mailbox

STORYTIME

Storytime

Literacy Ideas for Teachers®

What Do You Do With a Tail Like This?

Written by Steve Jenkins

Discover how different critters use their noses, ears, tails, and other body parts in this fun nonfiction book!

ideas contributed by Tricia Kylene Brown
Bowling Green, KY

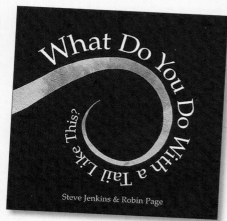

● ● ● What Do You Do? ● ● ●

Making connections
Before you read this story, have little ones point to their noses. Then say, "What do you do with a nose like this?" Prompt students to describe specific things they do with their noses, such as smell a flower, smell cookies that are baking, or blow them when they're runny. Then tell students that they're going to hear about unique things animals do with their noses and other body parts! Have students settle in for the read-aloud.

● ● ● Terrific Tails ● ● ●

Expanding the story through discussion
Get a length of crepe paper (tail) and give it to a child. Have a child hold the tail behind him and swish it back and forth. Then ask, "What would you do with your tail?" Prompt a child to use his imagination to describe how he would use his tail. Then have him give the tail to a classmate to repeat the process.

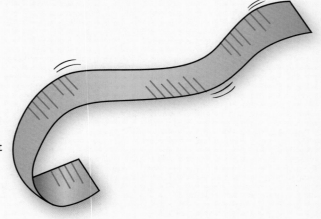

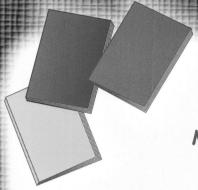

My Crayons Talk
by Patricia Hubbard

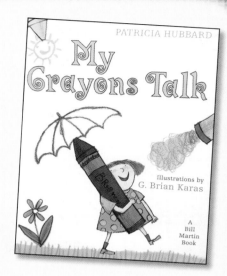

From purple bubble gum to brown mud pies, this book takes a lively look at crayons and colors—complete with rhythmic language galore!

ideas contributed by Cindy Hoying
Centerville, OH

> The yellow crayon would say that it's really happy!

● ● ● Can They Talk? ● ● ●
Speaking, creative thinking

Open a box of crayons and have little ones look inside. Then ask, "Can crayons talk?" Youngsters will surely giggle at this question! Next, choose a crayon and ask, "What do you think the [color] crayon would say if it could talk?" Listen to their suggestions. Then have little ones settle in for a story in which crayons do talk!

● ● ● Yackity, Clackity! ● ● ●
Identifying colors, playing a group game

Place crayons in a container. Then have students sit in a circle and give the container to a child. Have students recite the chant shown as they pass the container around the circle. At the end of the chant, have a child with the basket remove a crayon. Then encourage him to name the color of the crayon and something that is that color.

Talk, talk, my crayons talk.
Yackity clackity, talk, talk, talk!

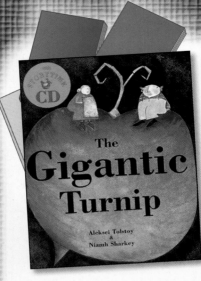

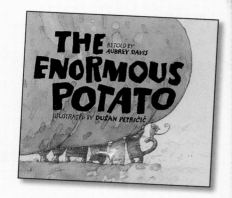

A BIG Book Battle:

The Gigantic Turnip
Written by Aleksei Tolstoy

vs.

The Enormous Potato
Written by Aubrey Davis

Compare and contrast two versions of this traditional tale with these ideas!

ideas contributed by Cindy Hoying, Centerville, OH

● ● ● **Potato or Turnip?** ● ● ●

Recalling story details

In advance, place brown pom-poms (potatoes) and yellow pom-poms (turnips) in your sand table (or in a container of brown paper shreds). After a read-aloud of both stories, have a child choose a pom-pom from the "garden." If he chooses a potato, have him share a detail from *The Enormous Potato.* If he chooses a turnip, have him share a detail from *The Gigantic Turnip.* Repeat the process with other youngsters.

● ● ● **Vote For a Veggie!** ● ● ●

Forming an opinion

Cut out a supply of the cards on page 184 and gather two soup pots. Attach a potato card and a turnip card to separate pots. Reread the two stories or review them with your little ones. Have students decide which story is their favorite; then have each child choose a potato card or a turnip card accordingly. Encourage her to color the card and place it in the appropriate pot. After everyone has voted, help students count the votes and compare the numbers, using the words *more, fewer,* and *equal.* For an extra challenge, help youngsters make a tally chart of the votes.

● ● ● **As Big As...** ● ● ●

Comparing size

Review the picture of the huge potato (or turnip) and ask youngsters if they think it's bigger than a car. How about a house? A dinosaur? After a discussion comparing size, gather a small group of youngsters and give each child a copy of page 185. Have each child dip a pom-pom in brown paint (potato) or yellow paint (turnip). Then have her pat the pom-pom on her paper to make the desired vegetable. Next, have her dictate to finish the sentence and draw a corresponding object next to the vegetable.

My _turnip_ is as big as _a dinosaur_

Too Much Noise

Written by Ann McGovern
Illustrated by Simms Taback

Peter's house makes noise. His bed squeaks, his tea kettle whistles, and the leaves outside go swish, swish! When Peter goes to the wise man to ask for advice, the wise man tells him to put a variety of animals in his house. After all the animal noise, Peter appreciates the quiet noises he heard before!

Ideas contributed by Cindy Hoying, Centerville, OH

● ● ● What's in the House? ● ● ●

What animals live in Peter's house? Youngsters recall the details with a fun activity! Cut out a copy of the animal cards on page 186 and place them facedown on a table. Draw a simple house on a sheet of chart paper. After the read aloud, have a child flip a card and identify the animal. Have students recall whether the animal is one that stayed in Peter's house. If it is, have the child attach the card to the house. Continue until all the cards have been flipped. ***Recalling story details***

● ● ● More Houseguests! ● ● ●

Youngsters get to be the wise man with this writing activity! Give each child a sheet of construction paper labeled with the prompt shown. Help him trim the paper so it resembles a house. Then have him decide what animal he would put in Peter's house. Write the animal's name on the paper. Then have him draw the animal. If desired, bind the pages together to make a class book with the title "More Houseguests for Peter!" ***Writing***

If I were a wise man, I would put <u>an elephant</u> in the house.

Old Black Fly

Written by Jim Aylesworth
Illustrated by Steven Gammell

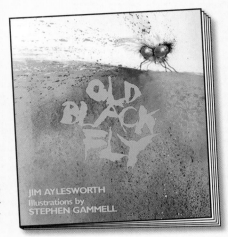

Old Black Fly buzzes through the alphabet as he annoys the inhabitants of a house in various ways. Finally, that annoying Old Black Fly meets his end with a SWAT!

Ideas contributed by Janet Boyce
Hinojosa Early Childhood and Pre-Kindergarten Center
Houston, TX

● ● ● A Fly Pointer ● ● ●

In advance, hot glue a black pom-pom (fly) to the end of a pipe cleaner to make a fun and bouncy pointer. After a read-aloud of the story, place the fly pointer and the book in the center. Encourage two students to look at the book. As one child "reads" the story, his classmate bounces the fly from page to page. *Developing book and print awareness, retelling a story*

● ● ● Swat Art! ● ● ●

Protect your art area and prepare a rolled-up newspaper by securing it with a rubber band. To begin, have a child draw Old Black Fly on a sheet of construction paper. Next, have her lightly dip the end of the rolled-up paper in a shallow container of paint and encourage her to swat the paper. Have her continue with other colors of paint. *Responding to a story through art*

Looking for a less-mess option? Fold the paper in half. Unfold the paper, have the child draw a fly, and then place dollops of paint on one half of the paper. Refold the paper and have her swat it with the rolled newspaper. Then have her unfold the paper to reveal the artwork!

Pumpkin Soup
by Helen Cooper

When Cat, Squirrel, and Duck make pumpkin soup together, everyone has a specific job. One day, Duck decides that he doesn't want to add the salt. Instead, he wants to stir the soup! When that results in a fight, Duck leaves. His friends search for him and regret not giving him a chance to stir. Then, when Duck comes back, all is forgiven!

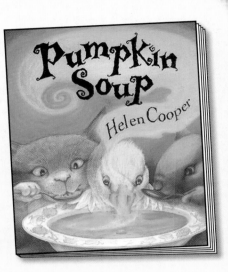

*Ideas contributed by
Cindy Hoying
Centerville, OH*

● ● ● Stir, Stir, Stir! ● ● ●

Have students sit in a circle. Then give a child a soup pot and spoon. Play a recording of music and have students pass the pot around the circle. Stop the music. Then ask the child with the pot a question related to the story. (See the options given.) After she answers, allow her to stir the "soup" like crazy—just as Duck did. Play several rounds of this fun game! *Speaking to answer a question about a story*

Suggested questions:
What do cat, duck, and squirrel like to make?
Where do they live?
Who adds the salt?
Who stirs the soup?
Who cuts the pumpkin slices?
Is Duck wrong to want to stir the soup? Why or why not?
Do you think Cat and Squirrel are good friends to Duck? Why or why not?
Why does Duck leave?
At the end, why don't Cat and Squirrel mind that Duck is stirring wrong?

● ● Pumpkin Soup Process Art ● ●

Youngsters re-create what the kitchen must have looked like after Duck's messy stirring experience! Dilute orange paint (pumpkin soup) and provide an eyedropper. Have a child use the dropper to drip and splatter pumpkin soup onto the paper from different heights. *Developing fine-motor skills, responding to a story through art*

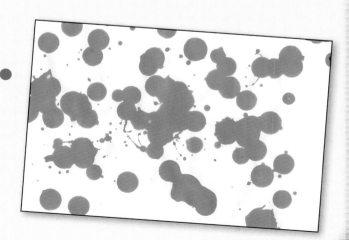

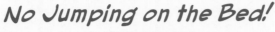

No Jumping on the Bed!
by Tedd Arnold

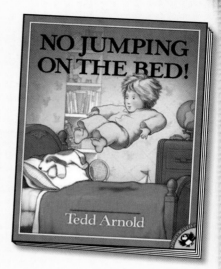

Walter's father insists that he stop jumping on the bed and go to sleep. When Walter does as he's told, he dreams that his jumping causes him to go through the floor to the apartment below his. That causes a hilarious chain reaction all the way to the basement of the building!

● ● ● Have You Jumped? ● ● ●
Making connections, gross-motor skills
Ask students if they know how to jump. You'll likely get an enthusiastic response! Next, have them demonstrate their jumping abilities. After several moments, have students sit down. Then ask if there are things that they are not allowed to jump on. Prompt students to name a few objects or locations that aren't appropriate for jumping. Then have students settle in for a story about a boy who does some enthusiastic jumping on his bed!

● ● ● Moving Walter ● ● ●
Taking part in an interactive rereading
In advance, draw a cross section of Walter's apartment building on a sheet of chart paper. You'll end up with eight floors, with Walter's apartment at the top and the basement at the bottom. Draw a simple Walter figure on a sticky note and have a child place it on the top floor. Then read the book aloud, having a child move the Walter figure from floor to floor when appropriate until it reaches the basement. After the read-aloud, have students determine the numbers for the floors and label them.

7
6
5
4
3
2
1
basement

Bear Stays Up For Christmas

Written by Karma Wilson
Illustrated by Jane Chapman

Bear's friends keep him moving so he can stay up for Christmas. But in the end, it's the friends that fall asleep, while Bear creates a fun Christmas for all!

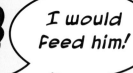
I would feed him!

● ● ● Wake Up! ● ● ●
Speaking to share opinions

Ask students how they would keep someone awake when that person wanted to fall asleep. After little ones share their thoughts, say, "Now let's pretend that you have to keep a bear awake. Would you keep a bear awake in a different way?" Have students consider that keeping a bear awake might be a bit more dangerous than trying to keep a friend or family member awake. Explain that the book you're about to read is about an extremely nice bear that wants to stay awake for Christmas!

● ● ● Preschoolers Stay Up ● ● ●
Contributing to a class book

Write the words shown on the bottom of the paper, leaving a blank for the pronoun. Then make a copy for each child. Have him write his name at the top of the paper. Then prompt him to decide something he would do the night before Christmas. Write his words after his name and fill in the appropriate pronoun. Then have him add an illustration to the page. Bind the pages together with a cover titled "Preschoolers Stay Up!" Read the book aloud during storytime.

Mikah shakes the presents under the tree.

But <u>he</u> still stays up!

The Mitten
by Jan Brett

Nicki loses one of his white mittens in the snow. One by one, a variety of woodland creatures crawl into the warm and cozy mitten. But when the mouse tickles the bear with her whiskers, the bear sneezes and the animals explode out of their warm resting place. Fortunately, Nicki gets his mitten back in the end.

I think ten will fit!

● ● ● How Many? ● ● ●
Measurement: area, estimating, counting

Youngsters will be intrigued to find out how many of them will fit on a supersize mitten! In advance, cut a mitten shape from white bulletin board paper (or an inexpensive shower curtain liner). Then place the giant mitten on your floor. Ask, "How many preschoolers will fit on the mitten?" Write down student guesses on a sheet of chart paper. Then have students count aloud as you prompt them to sit on the mitten, one at a time. When you can't fit any more preschoolers on the mitten, compare the final number to student guesses. Then have a child pretend to sneeze, prompting all the preschoolers to jump up quickly and go back to their seats.

Jenny Walser
Memories and Milestones
New Prague, MN

● ● ● Where Would It Sleep? ● ● ●
Recognizing fact from fiction

Make a copy of page 187 for each child. To begin, ask children whether they think the story is real or pretend. Lead youngsters to conclude that it is pretend because all those animals would not likely fit in a mitten nor would they want to take a nap together! Next, give each child a copy of page 187 and ask her where she thinks an owl would sleep in the real world. Have youngsters look at the pictures and color where they think an owl would likely sleep. Continue for each animal.

Tricia Kylene Brown
Bowling Green, KY

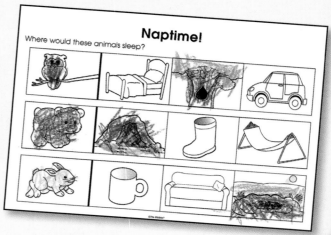

Naptime!
Where would these animals sleep?

The Little Engine That Could

by Watty Piper
Illustrated by Loren Long

When a happy train engine breaks down, a determined little replacement pulls a train full of toys to the boys and girls on the other side of the mountain.

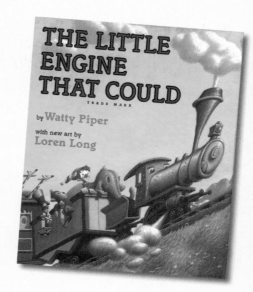

I help when I set the table.

● ● ● I Am Helpful ● ● ●
Speaking to share information

Gather youngsters and then write "I help…" on your board. Ask little ones to share ways that they help. Encourage each child to answer the question with a complete sentence beginning with the words "I help." Then ask, "How does it make you feel when you help someone?" Have youngsters share their thoughts. Then explain that the book you're about to read is about a train engine that helps.

Erin Buhr
Madison, MS

● ● ● I Think I Can ● ● ●
Listening, performing in an interactive read-aloud

Little ones will love this interactive rereading of the story! Get several rhythm instruments, such as tambourines, hand drums, and rhythm sticks. Then give each student an instrument and have him place the instrument on the floor in front of him. Next, reread the story. Whenever the train says, "I think I can," have youngsters play their instruments. After this read-aloud, keep a rhythm instrument handy. Whenever your students tackle challenging tasks, play the instrument and encourage them to chant, "I think I can. I think I can."

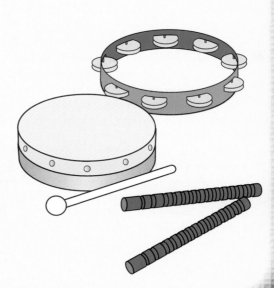

Guess How Much I Love You

Written by Sam McBratney
Illustrated by Anita Jeram

Little Nutbrown Hare loves Big Nutbrown Hare very much. As he describes his love in this enchanting tale, Little Nutbrown Hare discovers that he is loved even more.

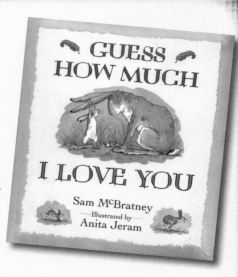

● ● ● Higher, Wider, Farther! ● ● ●
Introducing math vocabulary
Before reading the book, have little ones reach their hands high in the air. Then ask them if they can go even higher. Next, prompt them to move their arms to demonstrate wide and wider. Finally, ask a child to stand so she is far away. Then have a second child stand even farther. Have students settle in for this adorable story and encourage them to listen for words like *long, wide,* and *far.*

Erin Buhr
Madison, MS

● ● ● How Many Hearts? ● ● ●
Nonstandard measurement
Little Nutbrown Hare stretches out his arms as wide as they will go to show Big Nutbrown Hare how much he loves him. Have little ones measure their arm span to see how much love they have. Make a supply of heart cutouts and place them at the math center. Have a child stretch his arms as wide as possible. Then cut a length of yarn the exact length of his arm span. Instruct him to lay his yarn on the table or the floor. Then have him place hearts side by side above the yarn. Ask him to count the number of hearts he used. Now that's a lot of love!

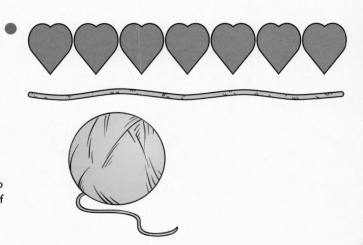

Animals in Winter

Written by Henrietta Bancroft and
Richard G. Van Gelder
Illustrated by Helen K. Davie

What do butterflies, woodchucks, squirrels, foxes, and other animals do during the winter? Youngsters find out with this informative and interesting nonfiction book.

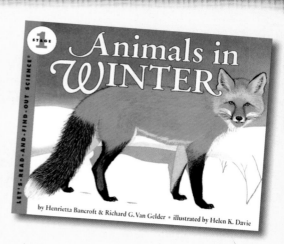

● ● ● Find and Tell ● ● ●
Recalling story details

Cut out a copy of the cards on page 188 and place them around the room so they can be easily seen. Have a child search for one of the cards. Give him hints, as needed, until he locates one. Then ask him to identify the animal and attach the card to a sheet of chart paper. Have students share details about the animal that they learned in the story. Repeat the process for each remaining animal card.

● ● ● Under the Snow ● ● ●
Investigating living things

In advance, place brown pom-poms (nuts) in your sensory table. Then place chunks of cotton batting and cotton balls (snow) over the nuts. Provide a container. Prompt little ones to recall how the squirrels buried nuts to save and eat over winter. Then encourage students to visit the center. Have little ones pretend they're squirrels and dig in the snow to get to the nuts. Then have them place the nuts in the container.

Erin Buhr
Madison, MS

Chickens to the Rescue

by John Himmelman

When Farmer Greenstalk and his family have various problems, who comes to the rescue? A flock of enthusiastic chickens! From finishing homework to getting a milk cow out of a tree, these chickens can do it all. And when the chickens are too tired, the farmer's pigs are eager to take their place!

ideas contributed by Janet Boyce
Hinojosa Early Childhood and Pre-Kindergarten Center
Houston, TX

Preschoolers to the rescue!

● ● ● Rescue? ● ● ●
Building vocabulary

What does it mean to *rescue* someone? Little ones decide with this prereading discussion! Show students the cover of the book and read the title aloud. Ask, "What does *rescue* mean?" Listen to several suggestions, leading students to understand that *rescue* means to save or help someone who is in trouble. Read aloud this hilarious book. Then, during center time throughout the next week, encourage students to be rescuers during dramatic play. Preschoolers to the rescue!

● ● ● Be the Chickens! ● ● ●
Taking part in an interactive read-aloud

During a second reading of the story, prompt little ones to be the chickens. Whenever you say the phrase "Chickens to the rescue!" prompt youngsters to join in as they jump up and flap their bent arms as if they were wings. When you get to the page that shows the sleeping chickens, prompt students to squat down and imitate the tired birds. Youngsters will love this active retelling!

Duck on a Bike
by David Shannon

When Duck discovers a bike, he decides to hop on and take a ride. He rides past all of his barnyard friends and they think a variety of things about Duck. But when a lot of bikes are available, all the barnyard animals decide to give this bike-riding thing a try!

● ● ● What Is Duck Thinking? ● ● ●
Dictating information to be written down, predicting
Open the book to the title page and have students look at the picture of Duck staring at the bike. Ask students what they think Duck is thinking. Then write their ideas on sticky notes and have the students attach the notes to the page. Next, read the story aloud to see if Duck acts on these thoughts.

● ● ● Clothesline Storytime ● ● ●
Putting story events in order
In advance, string a clothesline between two chairs and provide a container of spring-style clothespins. Cut out a copy of the picture cards on page 189. (If desired, laminate them for durability.) Then place the cards and the book near the clothesline. During center time, encourage students to visit this center and attach the animal cards to the clothesline in story order. Have them use the book as a reference.

Hattie and the Fox

Written by Mem Fox
Illustrated by Patricia Mullins

When a nose pokes through nearby bushes, Hattie alerts her uninterested farm friends. As the hidden animal slowly reveals itself, she becomes increasingly agitated, but her friends continue to disregard the situation—that is until Hattie declares that the animal is a fox!

Hattie is upset!

● ● ● The Look ● ● ●
Speaking, predicting
What is Hattie looking at? Youngsters guess with this prereading activity! Show students the cover of the book and have them focus on Hattie the hen. Ask them to predict whether Hattie is happy, angry, surprised, or upset. Then have students discuss what Hattie might be looking at. Before reading the book aloud, open the book so youngsters can see the fox on the back cover. So that's why she looks upset!

● ● ● What's in the Bushes? ● ● ●
Beginning sound /h/
Have little ones notice that *Hattie* and *hen* begin with /h/. Prompt little ones to put hands in front of their mouths to feel the air as they say /h/. Ask, "What if Hattie only saw things in the bushes that begin with /h/?" Prompt a child to name something that begins with /h/, such as *hamburger, ham, horn, hot dog, hummingbird, hippo, hanger, horse, helicopter, house,* or *hat.* Then reread the first page of the book, replacing the word *nose* with the suggested /h/ word. After the giggles die down, repeat the activity again.

I can see a hippo in the bushes!

The Tiny Seed
by Eric Carle

Seeds fly on the wind and land on the ground. Some of the seeds do not survive. But the tiny seed does. The tiny seed grows into a giant flower. And then one day the flower begins to lose its petals and the wind takes its seeds to scatter them over the land.

● ● ● Where Do Flowers ● ● ● Come From?
Investigating living things

Take youngsters outside and have them view a flower bed (or show them pictures of flowers). Invite students to share their thoughts about how they believe the flowers have grown where they did. After the discussion, read aloud Eric Carle's book *The Tiny Seed*. After the read-aloud, ask, "How did the flower get there?"

Janet Boyce
Hinojosa Early Childhood and Pre-Kindergarten Center
Houston, TX

● ● ● Eric Carle Did It All! ● ● ● ●
Reinforcing the jobs of authors and illustrators

Explain to students the jobs of author and illustrator. Then tell them that some books are written and illustrated by different people, but *The Tiny Seed* was written and illustrated by the same person: Eric Carle. To help them remember, lead them in singing the song shown.

(sung to the tune of "Mary Had a Little Lamb")

Eric Carle wrote the words,
Wrote the words, wrote the words.
Eric Carle wrote the words.
That's what an author does.

Eric Carle made the art,
Made the art, made the art.
Eric Carle made the art.
That's what an illustrator does.

My Garden
by Kevin Henkes

If a little girl had a garden of her own, it would grow seashells, glowing strawberries, patterned sunflowers, and more exciting and unique treasures!

ideas contributed by Cindy Hoying, Centerville, OH

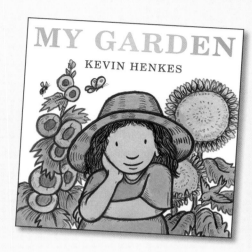

● ● ● **My Special Garden** ● ● ●
Speaking to answer a question
Youngsters decide what they would like in their own special gardens! After reading the book, hand a flower (real or artificial) to a child and recite the chant shown. Encourage the child to name something she might have in her special garden. Then have her give the flower to a classmate. Repeat the process until each child has had a turn.

[Student name, student name], what would you do
If there was a special garden for you?

● ● ● **Fun With Flowers!** ● ● ●
Responding to the story through art
Take a photo of each child with his arms outstretched, similar to the little girl in the book when she is surrounded by flowers. Help him cut out his photo and glue it to the middle of a sheet of paper. Then have him dab bingo daubers all around his photo. Next, have him draw stems, leaves, and petals so it appears as if he's surrounded by flowers.

To Market, To Market

Written by Anne Miranda
Illustrated by Janet Stevens

In this twist on the traditional rhyme, a woman goes to the market to buy a fat pig. She takes the pig home and returns to get a hen. But when she takes the hen home, the pig has gotten loose! The rhyme continues until she has a house full of animals running amok. It's much easier to buy vegetables and make soup!

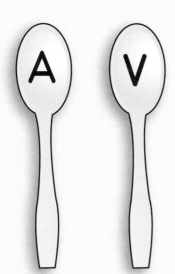

● ● ● Animal or Vegetable? ● ● ●
Categorizing

This story has a variety of animals and vegetables. Little ones categorize the items with simple spoons! Give each child a plastic spoon labeled "A" and a second spoon labeled "V." Then name an item from the story. Prompt students to decide whether the item is an animal or a vegetable. Then prompt them to hold up the corresponding spoon!

● ● ● Odd Headwear ● ● ●

Responding to a story through song, recognizing body parts

Turn to the page of the story that shows the duck on the woman's head. Show the picture to your students. Discuss with students if it would be fun to have a duck on one's head. Next, give each child a duck cutout (see the patterns on page 190). Then lead students in singing this song about an unruly duck, prompting them to place their ducks on the correct body part.

(sung to the tune of "If You're Happy and You Know It")

There's a duck on my [head], on my [head]. Quack, quack!
There's a duck on my [head], on my [head]. Quack, quack!
What a funny thing to see.
I think that you'll agree.
There's a duck on my [head], on my [head]. Quack, quack!

Continue with the following: *knee, hand, arm, shoulder, nose, thigh, foot, elbow, ankle*

Potato and Turnip Cards
Use with "Vote for a Veggie!" on page 168.

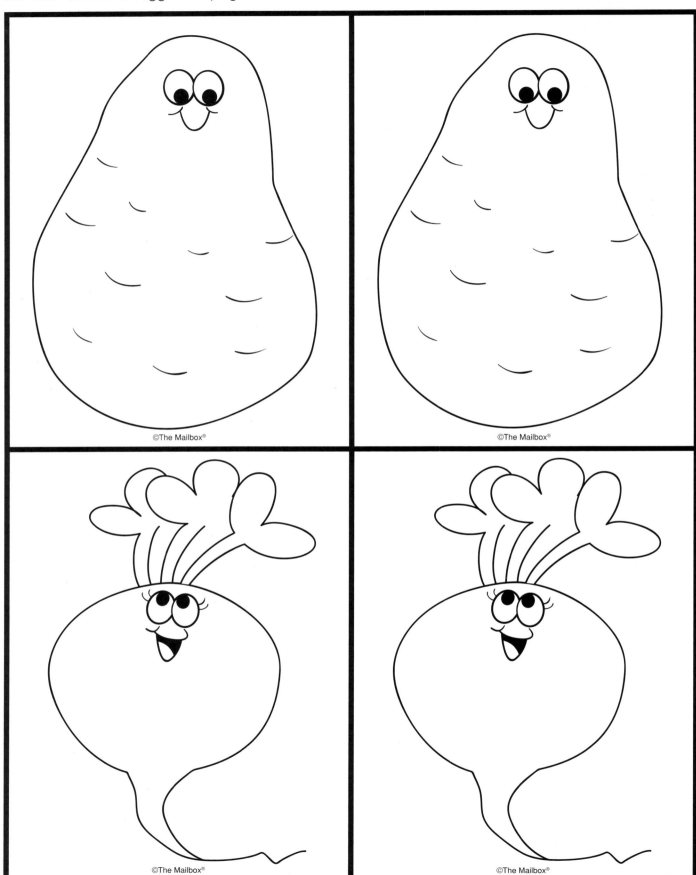

©The Mailbox®

©The Mailbox®

©The Mailbox®

©The Mailbox®

My _____ is as big as _____ .

©The Mailbox®

Note to the teacher: Use with "As Big As..." on page 168.

THE MAILBOX | 185

Animal Cards

Use with "What's in the House?" on page 169.

©The Mailbox®

©The Mailbox®

©The Mailbox®

©The Mailbox®

©The Mailbox®

©The Mailbox®

©The Mailbox®

©The Mailbox®

©The Mailbox®

©The Mailbox®

©The Mailbox®

©The Mailbox®

Naptime!

Where would these animals sleep?

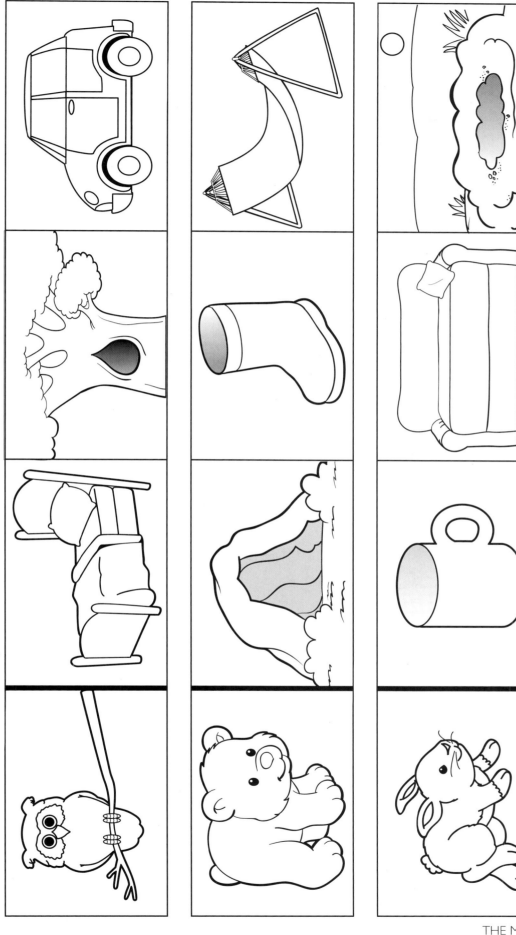

©The Mailbox®

Note to the teacher: Use with "Where Would It Sleep?" on page 174.

monarch butterfly

©The Mailbox®

squirrel

©The Mailbox®

woodchuck

©The Mailbox®

rabbit

©The Mailbox®

bluebird

©The Mailbox®

mouse

©The Mailbox®

©The Mailbox®
©The Mailbox®
©The Mailbox®
©The Mailbox®
©The Mailbox®
©The Mailbox®
©The Mailbox®
©The Mailbox®
©The Mailbox®

Duck Patterns
Use with "Odd Headwear" on page 183.

LITERACY UNITS

Ripe and Juicy Literacy Ideas!

Check out this sweet selection of watermelon-themed activities.

ideas contributed by Cindy Hoying, Centerville, OH

Add a Watermelon
Beginning sound /w/

Youngsters make a garden overflowing with watermelons! Get a sheet of brown paper (garden) and green pom-poms (watermelons). Then gather a small group of youngsters around the props. Name a word (see suggestions below). Then have little ones decide if the word begins with the /w/ sound. If it does, have a child place a watermelon in the garden. If it doesn't, youngsters do nothing. Continue in the same way until all the watermelons are in the garden.

Suggested words: *want, jump, wagon, wall, fun, cake, wash, waffle, sand, wand, warm, bear, watch, waist*

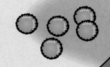

Syllables and Seeds
Counting syllables

Draw a watermelon slice on a sheet of chart paper and color it in as desired. Display the chart paper in your circle time area. Give a thick black marker to a child. Then name one of the words below. Have the child tap the marker on the watermelon slice as she says the word so that the resulting marks on the melon look like seeds. Help her identify the number of syllables in the word. Then have the remaining students clap the word. Continue with each remaining word until the slice is full of seeds!

Suggested words: *watermelon, juicy, ripe, seeds, yummy, vine, tasty, green, big, humongous, red, slice, drippy, sweet, melon, delicious*

Wonderful Watermelon

Developing print awareness, high-frequency word *it*

Make a copy of the booklet pages on page 195 for each child. Encourage each youngster to color the pages and cut them out. Then have her glue them to a 6" x 18" strip of red construction paper, accordion-folded. Label a front cover with the title shown and prompt her to sign her name. Then attach the front cover and a similar back cover. Help her "read" her booklet, encouraging her to point to the word *it* on each page.

Wonderful Watermelon by Lauren

Grow it. Pick it. Slice it. Eat it. Yum!

Let's Make Ws!

Forming W

Lead youngsters in singing the simple song shown. Each time they sing the word *watermelon*, encourage them to draw a letter W in the air, moving their finger down, up, down, and up again on the four syllables of *wa-ter-mel-on*. If desired, encourage them to sing the song as they practice forming Ws in a sand tray as well.

(sung to the tune of "Good Night, Ladies")

Watermelon,
Watermelon,
Watermelon
Begins with W!

In my garden, next to a weed,

I dug a hole to plant a O .

Pour some water—that was fun!

The seed will need the yellow ☼ .

My seed did sprout—it looked so fine.

It grew into a long green .

My watermelon is big and round.

It's time to pick it from the .

My sweet watermelon is so nice!

Do you want to eat a 🍉 ?

Story of a Watermelon

Rhyming, reading a rebus chant

On sentence strips, write the chant shown and place the strips in your pocket chart. Display a cutout copy of the cards from page 196 nearby. To begin, have students name the pictures. Then read aloud the first couplet, following the words with your finger. Encourage students to provide the final rhyme in the couplet. Then have a child find the matching picture and place it in the chant. Continue with each remaining picture.

Dripping Watermelon

Participating in a rhyming song

Guide students in singing this giggle-worthy sing-along!

(sung to the tune of "Head and Shoulders")

Watermelon on my face, on my face.
Watermelon on my face, on my face.
It is dripping, dripping everyplace!
Watermelon on my face, on my face.

Watermelon on my nose, on my nose.
Watermelon on my nose, on my nose.
It is dripping, dripping down it goes!
Watermelon on my nose, on my nose.

Watermelon on my chin, on my chin.
Watermelon on my chin, on my chin.
It is dripping, and it makes me grin!
Watermelon on my chin.

Watermelon Masterpiece!

Identifying letter W

Trim a sponge into a semicircle and place it near a shallow pan of pink or red paint. Also provide green paint and paintbrushes. Place a stack of letter cards with several Ws facedown. Gather a small group of children and give each child a sheet of paper. Have a youngster take a letter card and identify the letter. If it's a W, have her say, "/w/, watermelon!" Then prompt her to make a sponge print on her paper and make a green line of paint as shown so it resembles a watermelon slice. Continue the activity until each child has several slices on her paper. If desired, when the paint is dry, have each child use a black permanent marker to draw seeds.

Grow it. 1

©The Mailbox®

Pick it. 2

Slice it. 3

Eat it. Yum! 4

Rebus Cards
Use with "Story of a Watermelon" on page 193.

©The Mailbox®

©The Mailbox®

©The Mailbox®

©The Mailbox®

©The Mailbox®

A Bushel of Literacy Activities!

Harvest a lot of learning with this selection of whole-group and center-time activities!

Where Is B?

Letter-sound connections

Combine sign language, music, and literacy with this whole-group activity! To begin, teach little ones the American Sign Language hand signs for two or three letters you have studied in your classroom. Then lead them in performing the song shown, inserting one of the letter names. Repeat the song for each remaining letter. As youngsters learn more letter names throughout the school year, revisit the song.

(sung to the tune of "Where Is Thumbkin?")

Where is [B]? Where is [B]?
Here I am! Here I am!
Can you make the [B] sound? Can you make the [B] sound?
[/b/, /b/, /b/, /b/, /b/, /b/].

Put dominant hand behind back.
Bring out hand and make the letter sign.

Shake hand making sign.

Gerri Primak
Holden, MA

Loud and Quiet

Recognizing the difference between uppercase and lowercase letters

Gather uppercase and lowercase alphabet cards. Then place the uppercase alphabet cards in the top half of your pocket chart and the lowercase alphabet cards in the bottom half of your pocket chart. Point to each of the uppercase letters as little ones sing the "Alphabet Song" loudly. Then point to the lowercase letters as students sing the song quietly. Next, remove the lowercase letters. Replace some of the uppercase letters in the chart with lowercase letters. Then have them sing the song, encouraging them to sing loudly on the uppercase letters and quietly on the lowercase letters. What fun!

Margaret Aumen
Emory United Methodist Nursery School
New Oxford, PA

Lumpy, Bumpy, and Funny!

Using descriptive words

Gather three unique looking gourds. Sit the gourds in the middle of your circle time area and gather youngsters around. Lead students in singing the song shown. Then call on a child to pick up a gourd and describe something about it. Sing the song again and then repeat the process. After several rounds, display the gourds in a center with magnifying glasses for individual exploration.

(sung to the tune of "Sing a Song of Sixpence")

Gourds are grown like pumpkins all along a vine.
They look kind of silly sitting in a line.
Some are green and pointy and others orange and fat.
But people do not eat them. So what do you think of that?

The Weekly Storyteller

Developing print and book awareness, building confidence

Each week, choose a different book to read that is related to your current classroom theme. Read the book aloud several days in a row. Then, on the final day of the week, have a child "read" the story to his classmates. What a neat way to promote reading with confidence!

Amber Dingman
Play 'n' Learn Family Child Care and Preschool
Sterling, MI

Potato Prints

Recognizing letter P

Your little ones will love using potato prints to show their mastery of letter *P*! Prepare shallow containers of colorful paint. Place half of a small potato next to each container. (To make potato halves easier for little ones to grip, cut them as shown.) Gather a small group of students and show each child a letter *P* card. Explain that *P* says /p/ and that the word *potato* begins with *P*. Next, give each child a copy of page 200 and have her point to a *P* on her paper. Then have her make a colorful potato print over the *P*. Continue in the same way until youngsters have found all the *P*s.

Letter Clothesline

Forming letters, identifying letters, fine-motor skills

Suspend a rope between two chairs to make a clothesline. Cut small squares of fabric and use a permanent marker to write a different letter on each one. Then place the squares in a basket along with spring-style clothespins. A youngster visits the center and chooses a fabric square. Then she traces the letter and identifies it if she can. Finally, she attaches it to the clothesline.

A Menagerie of Syllables!

Clapping syllables

Lead students in reciting this chant slowly, encouraging them to clap the animal names. Repeat the chant several times, replacing the underlined words with a different action. (See the suggestions below.)

Hearing syllables is easy to do.
Let's [clap our hands] to hear a few!
Elephant, donkey, kangaroo,
Hippopotamus, tiger, emu!

Continue with the following: *stomp our feet, pat our tummies, pat our legs, wiggle our hips*

Suzanne Moore
Tucson, AZ

Lights Out!

Rhyming

Here's a flashy idea to entice students to discriminate between rhyming and nonrhyming words! First, make a darkened space by draping a large blanket or sheet over a long table. Ask a small group of youngsters to join you under the table; then give each of them a small flashlight. Have everyone turn on their flashlights. Direct the group to listen as you say a series of words. When the children hear a word that doesn't rhyme with the rest, they should turn off their flashlights! When the giggles subside, have everyone turn on their flashlights again; then begin with a new series of words.

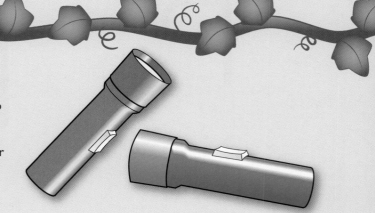

Potato Painting

Note to the teacher: Use with "Potato Prints" on page 198.

Clap and Color

©The Mailbox®

Note to the teacher: Have each child point to the picture in the first box and name it. Then have her clap the syllables as she names the picture again. Direct her to color a circle for each syllable. Repeat with each remaining box.

Phonological Awareness at Center Time

These centers all incorporate phonological awareness skills, which set your little ones up to be successful future readers!

ideas contributed by Roxanne LaBell Dearman
NC Intervention for the Deaf and Hard of Hearing, Charlotte, NC

Toss and Clap
Gross-Motor Area

Gather items with names that have one, two, or three syllables. (See the suggestions below.) Sort them into three containers and then put the containers on the floor in a traffic-free area. Place a pile of beanbags several feet away. A child tosses a beanbag, attempting to get it into one of the containers. When she does, she chooses an item from the container and names the item. Then she sets the item aside and claps its name. Youngsters continue until all the items have been removed from the containers. *Clapping syllables*

Suggested items:
One syllable—shoe, block, key, book
Two syllables—crayon, pencil, napkin, feather
Three syllables—banana, envelope, butterfly (image or toy)

Ba-na-na!

Pat, Pat the Cat
Play Dough Center

Cut out and laminate a copy of the picture cards on page 204. Then place the cards in your play dough center. A child visits the center and chooses a card. Then she places play dough on the picture and pats it in place while saying, "Pat, pat the [picture name]—just like that!" Then she removes the play dough and repeats the activity with another picture. *Reinforcing rhyming words*

Long Drive and Short Drive
Math Center

In advance, attach a strip of masking tape to your floor so it resembles a road. Provide student photos and toy cars. A child chooses a photo and names the classmate. Then she says the classmate's name slowly as she drives a car along the road, stopping at the end of the name. She continues with other classmates' names, noticing that some names are longer and the cars go farther. ***Reinforcing that words are made up of sounds, comparing length***

Bag or Mitten?
Literacy Center

Which items belong in bags and which belong in mittens? Youngsters can tell by the item's beginning sound! Gather a few items that begin with /m/ and a few that begin with /b/, such as macaroni, a map, a picture of the moon, a toy mouse, a small box, a bow, a bell, and a ball. Provide a mitten for each item that begins with /m/ and a paper lunch bag for each item that begins with /b/. Place the props at a center. A youngster chooses an item and says its name. If it begins with /m/, he places it in a mitten. If it begins with /b/, he places it in a bag. He continues until all the items are concealed! ***Matching beginning sounds***

One "Bapple," Please!
Dramatic-Play Area

In advance, gather play food and a plastic or paper plate. Gather youngsters. Hold out the plate and request a food, using a nonsense rhyming word instead of the food name. (For example, say, "I would like a 'bapple,' please.") When the giggling dies down, a child gives you an apple. Play continues until all the foods have been requested. For extra fun, encourage youngsters to request different foods in the same way! ***Rhyming***

Picture Cards

Use with "Pat, Pat the Cat" on page 202.

©The Mailbox®

©The Mailbox®

©The Mailbox®

©The Mailbox®

Let's Listen to WORDS

Look no further for appropriate and playful ideas that are just perfect to help your little ones hear the sounds in words.

Sing About It

Lead little ones in singing this song to help them understand that words are made up of different sounds. Sing the first verse. Then ask students to help you make a word. Say, "/k/, /a/, /t/" and help students blend the sounds to say *cat*. Then lead them in singing the second verse. Continue with other verses, using other simple words, such as *dog, net, cake, rock,* and *bell.*

(sung to the tune of "The Farmer in the Dell")

Let's listen to some words.
Let's listen to some words.
Words are made of different sounds.
Let's listen to some words.

[/k/, /a/, /t/], cat.
[/k/, /a/, /t/], cat.
Words are made of different sounds.
[/k/, /a/, /t/], cat.

Cooking Up Words

Gather a mixing bowl; a large spoon; a pie tin; and several manipulatives, such as counters or small blocks. Explain to students that you're going to bake some words! Choose a food word that has more than one syllable. Then say the word aloud, putting a manipulative into the bowl for each syllable. Have a child stir the manipulatives as you lead the class in chanting the syllables. Then have the child stop stirring, dump the manipulatives into the pie pan, and blend the syllables to form the word, with help as needed.

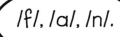

Mystery Word

Bring on the smiles with a cute puppet and this catchy tune! Use a puppet of your choice to sing the song. At the end of the verse, have the puppet say a familiar word in segments. Help students blend the sounds together and then say the word. Repeat the song with other words as time allows.

(sung to the tune of "The Farmer in the Dell")

Do you know my word?
Oh, do you know my word?
Put the parts together now,
And then you'll know my word!

Sound Train

All aboard for this small-group activity! Make enough copies of the train workmat on page 209 for each child in the group plus one for yourself. Also cut out a copy of the picture cards on page 208. Give each child four counters and a workmat. Next, show youngsters a picture card and have them name it. Help little ones segment the sounds in the word. Demonstrate how to place a counter on each box on the workmat for each sound heard and then say the blended word. Encourage youngsters to segment and blend the word again before removing their counters. Repeat the activity with the remaining picture cards.

Can You Guess?

Everyone gets to join in with a circle-time guessing game! In advance, place in a bag several items whose names have three or four sounds. Decide on one object in the bag and sing the song to the class. At the end of the song, say the segmented name of the object. Encourage little ones to blend the sounds and name the object. When it is named correctly, invite a child to remove it from the bag. Repeat the activity until all items have been guessed.

(sung to the tune of "If You're Happy and You Know It")

Can you guess what I've got hidden in this bag?
Can you guess what I've got hidden in this bag?
If you listen for the word,
Tell me every sound you heard.
Then you'll know what I've got hidden in this bag!
/m/, /u/, /g/.

Sun.
Ssss–uuuu–nnnn.
Sun.

Stretch It Out

For this class activity, show students an oversize rubber band and demonstrate how it stretches. Tell them they will be stretching words just as you're stretching the rubber band. Place the band around both hands with your palms facing each other and the band taut but not stretched. Say the word *rat* while holding your hands still. Now say *rat* again, but this time, stretch the sounds as you stretch the rubber band outward *(rrrr-aaaa-t)*. Then bring your hands back to the starting position and again say *rat*. Direct youngsters to hold their hands in front of them and pretend they each have a rubber band. Call out a word and have them say it, repeat it while stretching their pretend bands, and then bring their hands back together and say the word again.

Picture Cards

Use with "Sound Train" on page 206.

©The Mailbox®

©The Mailbox®

©The Mailbox®

©The Mailbox®

©The Mailbox®

©The Mailbox®

©The Mailbox®

©The Mailbox®

©The Mailbox®

©The Mailbox®

©The Mailbox®

©The Mailbox®

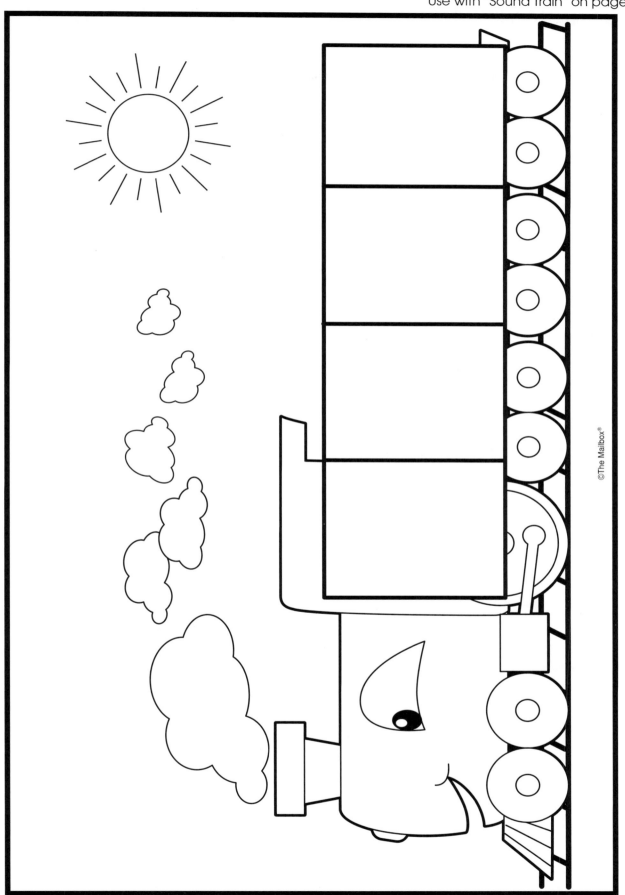

©The Mailbox®

Recognizing and Identifying Letters

Little ones will be enthusiastic about learning letter names with this collection of fun and engaging activities!

Secret Letters

Emphasize teamwork and cooperation with this literacy game! Gather pairs of small letter cards (or tiles). Then give each card to a child. As you hand them out, prompt children to hold them in their hands so classmates can't see and to whisper the name of the letter in your ear. Next, say, "Go!" and have students walk around showing their letter to their classmates. When a child finds the classmate who has the same letter he does, both of them sit down. When everyone is seated, have each pair show you their letters and tell you the letter name. *Identifying letters, matching letters*

Kimberly Papsin
Central Avenue Preschool
Naugatuck, CT

Letter Munch!

This activity is perfect for a letter review! Provide plastic dinosaur toys and letter blocks (or cards). Gather a small group of students and give each child a dinosaur. Hold up a letter block and have students name the letter. Give a child the block and have her make her dinosaur "eat" the letter, prompting her to make the letter sound as she does so. After each child has a chance, encourage students to name some words that begin with the letter, with help as needed. Repeat the process with other letter blocks. *Identifying letters, letter-sound association*

Cathy Mansfield
The Springhouse Learning Station
Eighty Four, PA

What's Missing?

Little ones will love being detectives to find the missing letter! Before students arrive for the day, remove one of the letters from your alphabet display and hide it in the room. If possible, hide it in or near something with a name that begins with that letter, such as placing the letter *S* in the sand table or letter *B* with the blocks. Then, when students notice that the letter is missing, prompt them to look for the letter throughout the day. When it is found, encourage youngsters to notice the connection between the letter and its location! *Identifying letters, beginning sounds*

Amy Aloi
Bollman Bridge Regional Early Childhood Center
Jessup, MD

Musical Letters

This twist on the game of musical chairs is particularly enjoyable because no one ever has to leave the game! In advance, place a class supply of chairs in a circle. Then attach large letter cards to the backrest of each of three chairs. Play music and have students walk in a circle. Then stop the music and prompt students to quickly find a seat. Have the children in the labeled chairs say the letter name and its sound. Then play another round! *Identifying letters, letter-sound association*

Martha Cymbaluk
Child-Parent Centers
Tucson, AZ

Letter Catch of the Day!

Label construction paper fish cutouts with different letters. (See page 213 for patterns.) Give a fish to each child and hold out a butterfly net (fish net). Then have a child name the letter on his fish, with help as needed, and toss it into the net. For extra fun, have a few fish jump out of the net, calling them by their letter names and claiming that they're trying to get away. Continue until all the letter fish are in the net. *Identifying letters*

Robin Kent
Avon Nursery School
Avon, MA

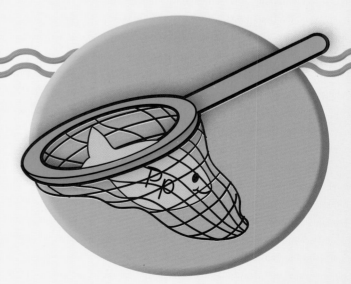

Letter Building

Cut out circles, semicircles, and strips from colorful construction paper and place them at a center. For extra fun, also provide wood shapes and pieces. Read aloud *Alphabet Under Construction* by Denise Fleming. Have students notice how the mouse is building and creating each letter. Then have students visit the center and use the pieces and strips to construct their initials or their names on a sheet of tagboard. ***Forming letters***

Marisol Carlos
Kidwatch Plus
Chicago, IL

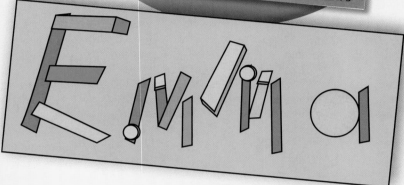

Sing a Song

Prepare a class supply of letter cards representing three or four of the letters you've been teaching. Give a card to each child. Then sing a round of the song shown, inserting a letter and sound and prompting the appropriate students to raise their cards. Continue with each remaining letter. ***Recognizing letters, letter-sound association***

(sung to the tune of "If You're Happy and You Know It")

If you're holding letter [S], raise your card. [/s/, /s/]!
If you're holding letter [S], raise your card. [/s/, /s/]!
Hold your letter [S] up high!
Hold it right up to the sky!
If you're holding letter [S], raise your card. [/s/, /s/]!

Roxann Norman
Fair Avenue Alternative Elementary
Columbus, OH

©The Mailbox®

©The Mailbox®

Let's Form Letters!

Get youngsters comfortable forming letters with these fun and unique ideas that are perfect for preschoolers!

Sticks and Stones

Here's a center that helps youngsters form letters as well as identify them. Draw a letter on a large piece of poster board and place it at a center along with a container of sticks and medium-size stones. Encourage youngsters to name the letter and trace it with their fingers. Then have them place sticks and stones over the letter. Little ones will love arranging the natural items!

Margaret Aumen
Emory United Methodist Nursery School
New Oxford, PA

Butterfly Letters

Literacy Center

On each of several sheets of construction paper, write a letter. Place the letter mats and a supply of brightly colored bow-tie pasta (butterflies) at a center. A child chooses a letter, names the letter, and then covers it with butterflies. She repeats the process with other letters.

Trace, Write, or Draw

Write uppercase and lowercase letter pairs on separate sheets of colorful paper. Laminate the sheets and then bind them to make a book. Place the book at a center along with dry-erase markers and an eraser. Youngsters can use this book all year long to practice tracing the letters, writing them, or drawing a picture that begins with the letter.

Hilda Cline
Petal, MS

MATH UNITS

Ahoy, Little Sailors!

Nautical Math Activities

Sailboats, sailors, anchors, and lighthouses—your little ones are sure to love these math activities!

 ### Anchors Aweigh!

Sorting, patterning

Your little sailors may not know that anchors come in different shapes! Make three circles with blue yarn and place a different anchor card (see page 218) in each circle. Then give each child an anchor card. Say, "Sailor [child's name], raise your anchor and place it in a circle!" Encourage the child to sort his anchor into the appropriate circle. Continue in the same way with each child, occasionally pausing to ask the youngster to explain why he sorted his anchor as he did. When finished, lead students in creating patterns with the anchors.

Roxanne LaBell Dearman
NC Intervention for the Deaf and Hard of Hearing
Charlotte, NC

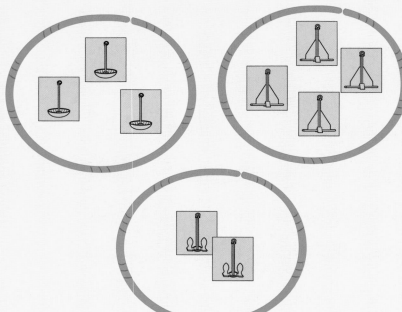

Nautical Knots

Counting, comparing, using the sense of touch

Cut same-size lengths of rope and make a different number of knots in each length. Then place the ropes in a center. Gather two students and have each child take a length of rope. Have her run her fingers over the rope and count the number of knots. Then have the students compare the numbers of knots, using words such as *more* and *less*. Finally, have them place the ropes back in the pile and then take two different ropes.

Cindy Hoying
Centerville, OH

A Lovely Lighthouse
Making a pattern with colors

Give each child a copy of page 219. Explain that a lighthouse gives off light to help ships know where they are. Then have each child choose two crayons and color her lighthouse to make an *AB* pattern. Prompt her to read her pattern aloud. Next, have her spread glue over the light and then sprinkle gold glitter over the glue. If desired, have the child cut out her lighthouse and glue it to a black sheet of paper.

Roxanne LaBell Dearman
NC Intervention for the Deaf and Hard of Hearing
Charlotte, NC

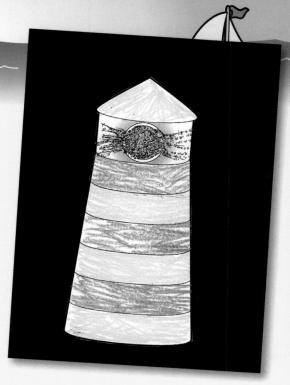

Building Ships
Exploring shapes, spatial skills

Attach a length of blue bulletin board paper to a table. Cut a supply of craft sticks in half and place them at the table along with pattern blocks in triangle and trapezoid shapes. Encourage youngsters to use the supplies to make a fleet of sailboats!

Cindy Hoying, Centerville, OH

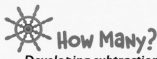
How Many?
Developing subtraction skills

This adorable fingerplay will be popular with your little sailors! Recite the rhyme five times, reducing the numbers by one each time. (During the final recitation, tweak the words as needed to work with one and zero.)

[Five] little ships in the sea   *Hold up five fingers.*
Float so happily.   *Bob fingers up and down.*
One moves by,   *Bob one finger from left to right.*
And now I spy
[Four] little ships in the sea!   *Hold up four fingers.*

Cindy Hoying

Anchor Cards

Use with "Anchors Aweigh!" on page 216.

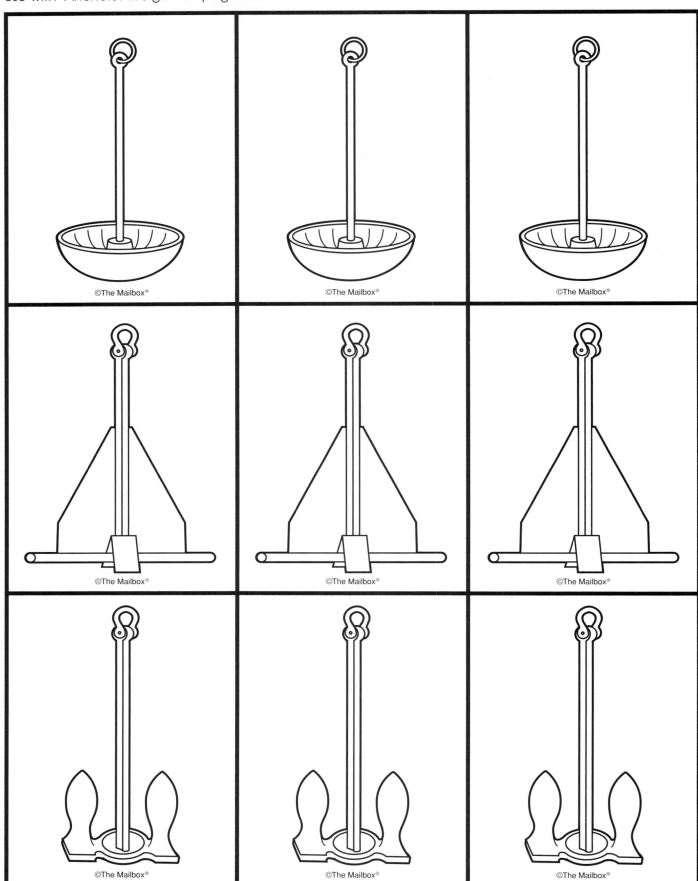

©The Mailbox®
©The Mailbox®
©The Mailbox®
©The Mailbox®
©The Mailbox®
©The Mailbox®
©The Mailbox®
©The Mailbox®
©The Mailbox®

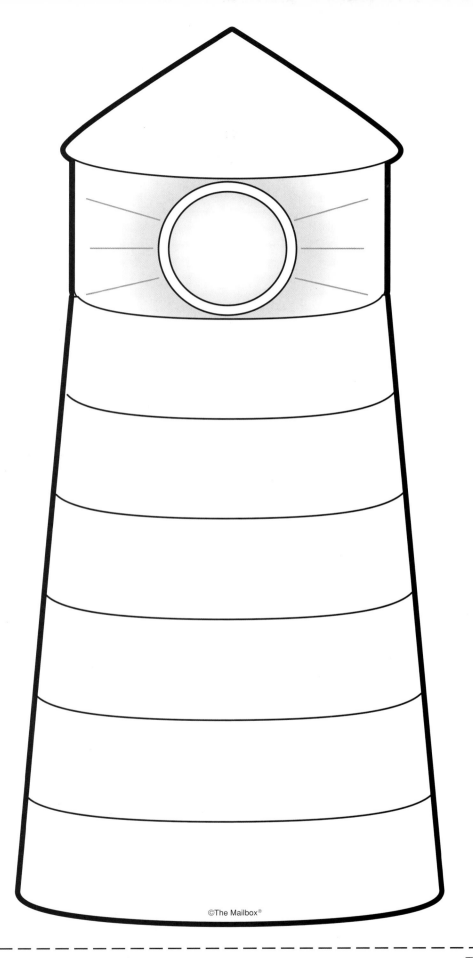

Note to the teacher: Use with "A Lovely Lighthouse" on page 217.

THE MAILBOX **219**

©The Mailbox®

Math With the Itsy-Bitsy Spider

Little ones will love math activities that focus on this popular classic song!

It's a Downpour!

Exploring volume

Your youngsters can make it rain in your water table! Poke holes in empty soda bottles and place them in your water table along with plastic spiders, containers in various sizes, and pieces of PVC pipe (waterspouts). Encourage youngsters to visit the center and explore the items, using the song as inspiration!

An Itsy-Bitsy Booklet

Counting eight items using one-to-one correspondence

In advance, cut out eight black construction paper strips (legs) for each child. To begin, have each child color and cut out a copy of the cards on page 222. Encourage her to sing the song and put the cards in order. Then staple the cards together at the top to make a flipbook. Next, have her count out eight legs, pointing to a different leg each time she says a different number name. When she has correctly counted eight legs, have her attach them to a black paper plate as shown. Then place glue on the final page of the booklet and glue it to the plate. If desired, have the child glue eye cutouts above the booklet. When the glue is dry, encourage her to sing the song and flip the pages of the booklet.

Cindy Hoying
Centerville, OH

Spiders Up the Spout

Developing subtraction skills

Lead little ones in this neat fingerplay that encourages early subtraction skills! Have youngsters sing the first verse. Then repeat the verse four more times, tweaking the words as necessary for the final verse.

(sung to the tune of "The Farmer in the Dell")

[Five] spiders up the spout,   *Wiggle five fingers.*
[Five] spiders up the spout,   *Wiggle five fingers.*
It rained and washed one out!   *Wiggle all fingers downward.*
[Four] spiders up the spout.   *Hold up four fingers.*

Cindy Hoying
Centerville, OH

Itsy-Bitsy's Friends

Sorting by size

All these spiders get to experience washing out of the waterspout before being sorted! Get a large cardboard tube and small, medium, and large pom-poms (spiders). Put the spiders in a container. Then place three separate hoops (or yarn circles) on the floor. Label the hoops "small," "medium," and "large." A child closes his eyes and reaches into the container to choose a spider. He opens his eyes and decides if his spider is small, medium, or large. Then he stands over the appropriate hoop and drops his spider through the waterspout. Continue until all the spiders have been sorted into the hoops.

Cindy Hoying

The Great Big Purple Spider

Recognizing colors

Youngsters will love this spider game! Cut out two copies of the spider cards on page 223. Then color each spider a different color. Place the cards on your floor and gather youngsters around. Lead them in singing the first two lines of the traditional song. Then say, "Next door to the Itsy-Bitsy spider lived a Great Big [color] spider!" Sing the first two lines of the song, inserting the name of the new spider. Then have a child find the card that shows the spider and flip it over. Continue until all the cards are flipped over.

Kelly Noll
Diamond Street Early Childhood Center
Akron, PA

Sequencing Cards

Use with "An Itsy-Bitsy Booklet" on page 220.

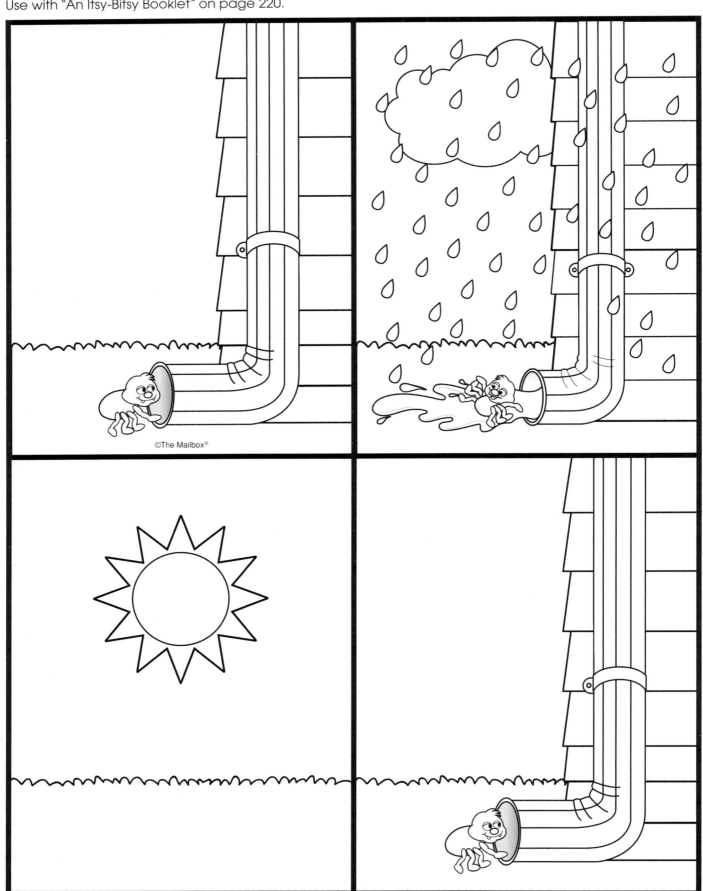

©The Mailbox®

©The Mailbox®

©The Mailbox®

©The Mailbox®

©The Mailbox®

Math With The Doorbell Rang

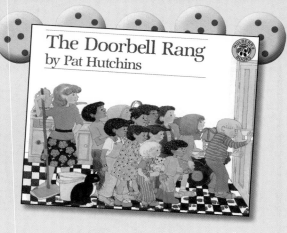

The Doorbell Rang
by Pat Hutchins

After a read-aloud of Pat Hutchins's classic story, reinforce math skills with these terrific activities!

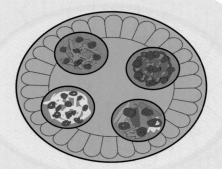

How Many?
Making equal sets
Gather a group of three youngsters and give each child a paper plate. Place 12 brown circle cutouts (cookies) on the table. Then tell students they need to split up the cookies so everyone gets the same amount. Once they divide the cookies evenly, have them use crayons to decorate the cookies as desired and then glue the cookies to their plates.

Sing a Song of Cookies
Counting, participating in a song
Review the plot of the story with a counting song! Give each child a strip of cookies from page 225. Then lead them in singing the first verse of the song shown as they point to each cookie. As they sing the second verse, have them clap to the beat.

(sung to the tune of "Ten Little Indians")

One, two, three, four, five little cookies;
Six, seven, eight, nine, ten little cookies;
Eleven and 12, that's all the cookies—
Twelve cookies to share.

Twelve little kids share 12 little cookies.
Twelve little kids share 12 little cookies.
Twelve little kids share 12 little cookies.
Grandma brings some more!

 You can also use the cookie strips for measurement and patterning!

What's in There?
Exploring volume
In advance, place a tub with flour and a separate tub with sugar at a center along with measuring cups and spoons. Ask little ones what Ma and Grandma probably use to make their cookies. After a brief discussion, explain to little ones that flour and sugar are two of the main ingredients in most cookie recipes. Then invite students to visit the center and use the measuring cups and spoons to explore the different items.

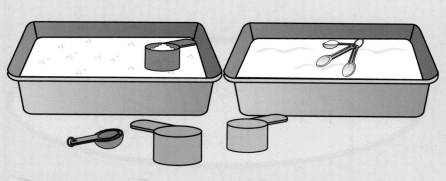

©The Mailbox®

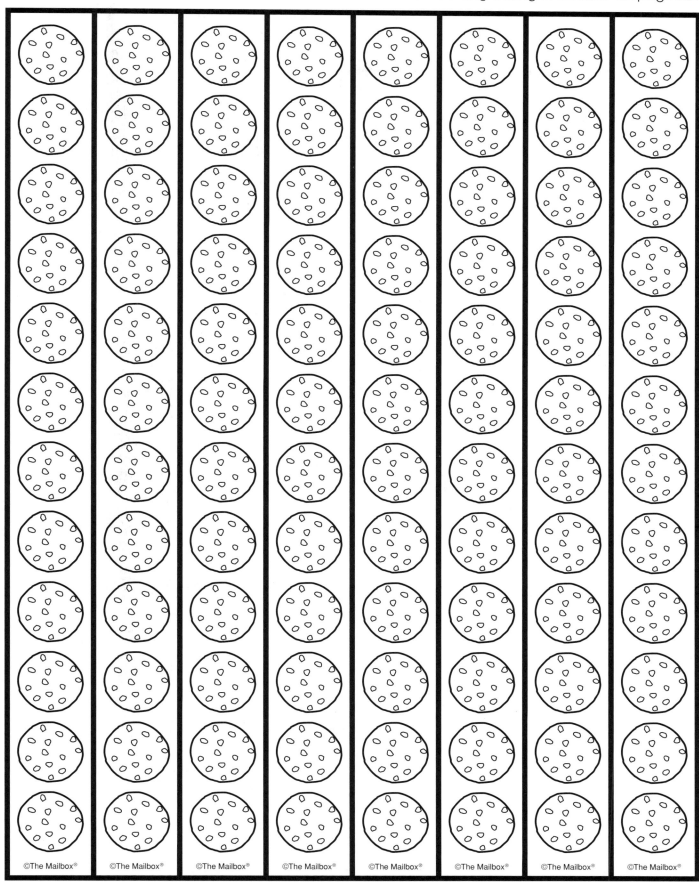

©The Mailbox®   ©The Mailbox®   ©The Mailbox®   ©The Mailbox®   ©The Mailbox®   ©The Mailbox®   ©The Mailbox®   ©The Mailbox®

Let's Talk About Time

Before, after, noon, nighttime, younger, and older—get little ones talking about these concepts of time and more.

ideas contributed by Cindy Hoying
Centerville, OH

I Rise Like the Sun

Concepts: morning, noon, nighttime

This relaxing little action chant helps build vocabulary. To begin, recite the chant for youngsters without the actions. Then ask, "What does *noon* mean?" Lead youngsters to conclude that *noon* is another word for 12:00 PM. This is a time when many people eat lunch. Next, have students perform the action chant.

I rise with the sun in the morning.	Stand and raise arms to make a circle.
I'm up like the sun at noon.	Stay in position.
I set like the sun at nighttime,	Slowly sit down while keeping arms raised.
And I sleep by the light of the moon.	Pillow hands under cheek and lie down.

How Young Are They?

Concepts: young, younger, youngest

Place old magazines in a center along with scissors and encourage students to cut out photos of children. After each youngster has had an opportunity to visit the center, gather the pictures. Then, during circle time, display two pictures of children who are different ages. Ask, "Which child is younger?" Have a student point to the child. Then add a picture of a child younger than the other two. Ask, "Which child is the youngest?" Continue playing this game with other pictures. If desired, play the game on another day using the terms *old, older,* and *oldest.*

What Order?

Concepts: before, after

Cut out a copy of the cards on page 228. Then place the picture showing the bed on the right side of your pocket chart. Lead students in singing the first verse of the song shown. Then have a child find the card with the hug and place it before the picture of the bed. Sing the second verse of the song, replacing the two different underlined phrases with the ones mentioned below. Then have a child find the book card and place it before the hug card. Continue with the next verse, having a child place the toothbrush card before the book card. Finally, lead them in the final verse, pointing to each card from left to right when indicated.

(sung to the tune of "For He's a Jolly Good Fellow")

Before I [sleep in my warm bed],
Before I [sleep in my warm bed],
Before I [sleep in my warm bed],
There's something that I do.
I [get a great big hug].
I [get a great big hug].
Before I [sleep in my warm bed],
I [get a great big hug].

Continue with the following:
get a great big hug/hear a story read
hear a story read/have to brush my teeth

Final verse:
Then after brushing my white teeth
and after hearing a book read
and after getting a big hug,
I sleep in my warm bed!

Clock or Calendar?

Understanding instruments used to measure time

Get a calendar and a clock and place them in your circle time area. Read one of the statements below. Then help students decide which tool would be better to use: a clock or a calendar.

- Lunch is at 1:00. What would I use to find out when it's 1:00?
- Valentine's Day is February 14. What would I use to find out when it's February 14?
- I'm going to a birthday party on Friday. What would I use to find out when it's Friday?
- I go to bed at 10:00. What would I use to find out when it's 10:00?
- I need to leave in 15 minutes. What would I use to keep track of 15 minutes?
- What day last week did I go to the grocery store? What would I use to find out?

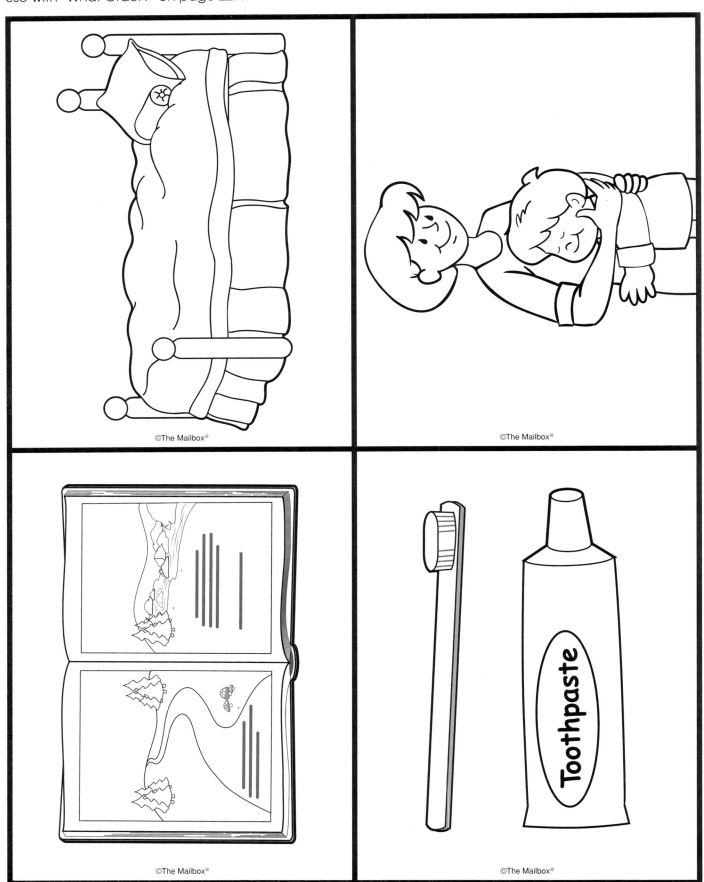

©The Mailbox®

©The Mailbox®

©The Mailbox®

©The Mailbox®

St. Patrick's Day Measurement

The luck of the Irish will be with you when you guide little ones through these marvelous measurement activities!

How Many Leprechauns?

Exploring area, estimating

Cut out a supersize yellow circle (gold coin) from bulletin board paper and place it on the floor. Gather name cards. Tell little ones that they're going to pretend to be leprechauns. Ask, "How many leprechauns do you think can fit onto this piece of gold?" Have students guess. If desired, write their estimates on the board. Then hold up a name card and say the chant shown. Prompt the leprechaun to do her best Irish jig over to the gold and then sit down on it. Continue until no more leprechauns can fit on the gold. Then help students count the leprechauns on the gold and compare the number to their estimates.

Leprechaun [student name], do as you're told, and dance your way to the leprechaun gold!

Short to Tall

Comparing height

In advance, make a copy of page 231 for each child. Have each student color the shamrocks and then cut out the cards. Next, encourage her to compare the heights of the shamrocks and place them in order on a 9" x 12" sheet of construction paper. After checking for accuracy, have her glue her shamrocks to the paper.

The Longest Beard!

Using measurement vocabulary

Lead little ones in performing a fun action song about a leprechaun named Paddy!

(sung to the tune of "Must Be Santa")

Who has a pot that's round and big?   Hold arms in a big circle.
Paddy has a pot that's round and big!
Who has short legs that dance a jig?   Dance a jig.
Paddy has short legs that dance a jig!
Pot that's big, dance a jig!   Repeat both moves.
He's a leprechaun, he's a leprechaun,   Clap to the beat.
He's a leprechaun, leprechaun!

Who has a beard that's long and red?   Move hand to show a long beard.
Paddy has a beard that's long and red!
Who wears a tall hat on his head?   Hold hand above head.
Paddy wears a tall hat on his head!
Long and red, hat on head!   Repeat both moves.
He's a leprechaun, he's a leprechaun,   Clap to the beat.
He's a leprechaun, leprechaun!

Looking for a golden measurement opportunity? Attach a row of sparkly gold pom-poms to jumbo craft sticks and place the resulting leprechaun gold measurement tools at a center. Encourage students to take a measurement tool and hold it up against items in the room to "measure" them!

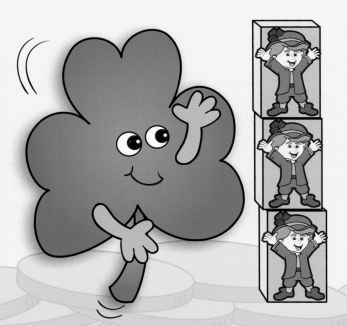

A Leprechaun Stack

Using nonstandard measurement

Who is taller: a preschooler or a leprechaun? Youngsters answer this question with an adorable activity! Cut out several copies of the leprechauns on page 45. Then glue each one to a building block. Have a child stand in front of the class. Then place a leprechaun block next to her. Have students decide who is taller: the preschooler or the leprechaun. Lead students to use descriptive words such as *taller* and *shorter*. Then say, "I wonder how many leprechauns we would have to stack to reach the height of a preschooler. Have students help you stack and count leprechaun blocks until they reach the height of the child. Then place the blocks in a center for independent practice.

Betty Silkunas
Lower Gwynedd Elementary
Ambler, PA

Super Sets of Ten!

Youngsters practice making and counting sets of ten, as well as sets of ten with extras!

ideas contributed by Cindy Hoying, Centerville, OH

Friendly Fingers

Little ones think about their fingers as a set of ten with this action song.

(sung to the tune of "The Farmer in the Dell")

Each finger is a friend.	*Wiggle the right hand.*
Each finger is a friend.	*Wiggle the left hand.*
Add them, and they make ten.	*Clap hands to the beat.*
Each finger is a friend.	*Wiggle both hands.*
Five fingers on each hand.	*Wiggle the right hand.*
Five fingers on each hand.	*Wiggle the left hand.*
Ten friends are really grand.	*Clap hands to the beat.*
Five fingers on each hand.	*Wiggle both hands.*

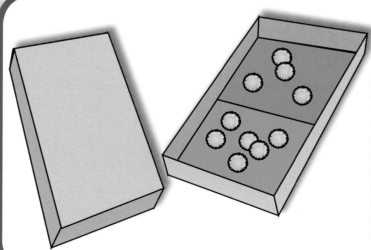

Buzzing Bees

What's the buzz? Sets of bees in the sky and in the grass! Get a lidded box and then attach a piece of blue construction paper and green construction paper to the inside bottom of the box as shown. To begin, have two youngsters count aloud as you place ten yellow pom-poms (bees) in the box. Put on the lid and have a child shake the box and buzz enthusiastically. Then have her place the box on the table and remove the lid. Prompt one child to count the bees in the sky and the second child to count the bees in the grass. Then have them count all the bees together. Play several rounds of this game!

Splat!

Cut out a supply of ice cream scoop patterns from page 234. Gather several number cards with numerals from 5 to 8 and place them facedown in a stack. Also place a brown paper cone shape on the floor. Tell students that the cone can hold only ten scoops and any extras will fall and go "splat"! Have a student choose a card, name the number, and then place that many scoops on the cone. Have a second child repeat the process. Then have students count the scoops on the cone. If there are more than ten, react with dramatic dismay and have students help you remove the extra scoops, saying, "Splat!" for each one. Reinforce the concept by pointing out the set of ten scoops with the number of extras. Then play again!

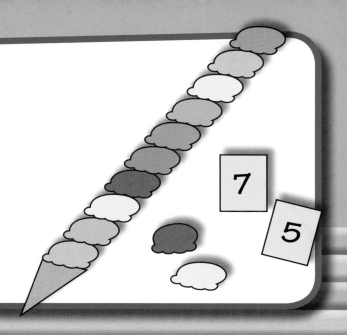

Totally Tubular

Develop hand-eye coordination as well as math skills with this center activity! Gather ten small cardboard tubes and an equal amount of Ping-Pong balls (or other small balls). Place the tubes, balls, and a tub at a center. Encourage youngsters to count to ten as they stand the tubes up in the tub. Next, have students count to ten as they place a ball in each tube!

On the Nose!

This talented seal can balance balls on its nose—but don't give it more than ten! Have each child cut out a copy of a seal pattern from page 235. Then have her glue it to the bottom of a 9" x 12" sheet of construction paper. Give her between ten and 13 sticky dots (balls). Explain that the seal can only balance ten balls on its nose. Then have her count as she places a set of ten balls above the seal, sticking any extra balls next to the seal. Lead her to notice that she made a set of ten with some extras.

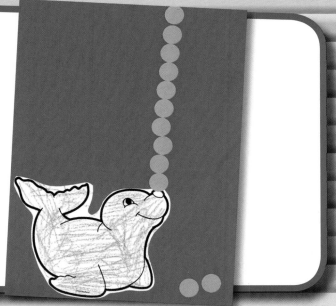

Ice Cream Scoop Patterns

Use with "Splat!" on page 233.

©The Mailbox®

©The Mailbox®

©The Mailbox®

©The Mailbox®

©The Mailbox®

©The Mailbox®

MATH in the Great Outdoors!

Take your little ones outdoors and into the sunshine for some marvelous math activities!

ideas contributed by Janet Boyce
Hinojosa Early Childhood and Pre-Kindergarten Center
Houston, TX

How Many Bees?

Sequencing numbers, counting

Inexpensive plastic flowerpots double as beehives! Turn ten plastic flowerpots upside down and label the bottoms with different numerals from 1 to 10. If desired, add a corresponding dot set to the bottom of each pot. Draw a chalk number line on the pavement and place the beehives nearby along with a supply of yellow pom-poms (bees). A youngster puts the beehives in order along the line. Then she pushes the corresponding number of bees in the drainage hole of each pot!

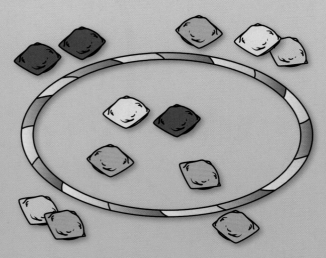

Jump, Frogs!

Comparing sets, positional words, gross-motor skills

With this activity, youngsters get practice with a variety of skills! Place a plastic hoop (pond) on the ground and have students stand in a very wide circle around the hoop. Give each child a beanbag (frog). Say, "Jump, frogs, jump!" and then have students toss their frogs to try to get them into the pond. Next, have students help you count the frogs in the pond and outside of the pond. Lead them in comparing the sets using the words *more* and *fewer*.

Lid Float

Counting, one-to-one correspondence

Bring your water table outside along with medium-size plastic lids and a large foam die. A child rolls the die and counts the dots. Then she floats that number of lids in the water table. For extra fun, provide plastic animal toys and have her place one on each lid.

Make a Caterpillar!

Adding sets by drawing

Gather a few children and give each child a piece of sidewalk chalk. Space the children out on the pavement and have them sit down. Then have each child draw a circle. Say, "Add one more circle next to the first one." Then have students count the circles. Continue instructing students to add circles and then count the total. Finally, prompt each youngster to draw antennae, legs, and a face to transform her circles into a caterpillar!

Paint With Water

Naming shapes by description, drawing shapes

Give each child a cup of water and a chunky paintbrush. Describe a shape, naming its number of sides and angles and a common object that is typically that shape. When students identify the shape, have them dip their paintbrushes in the water and "paint" the shape on the pavement. Continue with other shapes.

Planting Flowers

Identifying numbers, making sets

Little ones plant a lovely flower garden with this activity! Write numbers 1 to 5 on separate paint sticks. If desired, draw a matching number of dots on each stick. Push the sticks into the ground so that the numbers show. Provide a container of plastic flowers with sturdy stems. Students read a number. Then they push that many flowers into the ground behind the stick. Students repeat the process with each remaining stick.

Sort It Out

Sorting by attributes

Here's a sorting activity that combines attributes with playground fun. Gather a chart tablet and marker; then take your students to the playground. Slowly give clues that describe a particular piece of equipment or an activity on your playground, such as "You can slide on this." Have students think of the activity as it's described. Then encourage each child to go to the activity described when she knows the answer. Continue to describe the activity until it's apparent to all students. Discuss and record the name of the activity and the clues that made it clear to the majority of students. For more challenge, describe the equipment or activities with more difficult attributes, such as color, shape, or material.

Hoop Jump

Understanding that the last number said is the number in a set, gross-motor skills

Gather five plastic hoops and place them in a row. Have students sit in a row facing the hoops. Choose a youngster and tell him a number from 1 to 5. Then have the other students count aloud as he hops from hoop to hoop, until they reach the appropriate number. Continue with other youngsters.

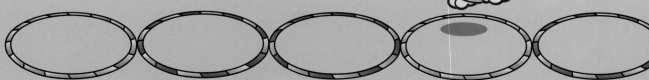

TEACHER RESOURCE UNITS

I Can Reach a Goal!

Perseverance

Help little ones understand the power of perseverance with activities on this important character trait!

That's Hard!

Participating in a song

Here's a catchy song that emphasizes sticking with a difficult task!

(sung to the tune of "If You're Happy and You Know It")

When there's something hard to do, I won't give up. (No way!)
When there's something hard to do, I won't give up. (No way!)
I will try and try again.
I'll hang tough and won't give in!
When there's something hard to do, I won't give up. (No way!)

Suzanne Moore
Tucson, AZ

Persistence Pudding

Following directions

This simple snack activity is terrific for teaching perseverance! For each child and yourself, place one tablespoon of instant pudding mix in a resealable plastic freezer bag. (Freezer bags are nice and sturdy!) Add one-fourth cup of milk to each bag and seal it securely. Encourage students to shake their bags as you shake yours. After a few seconds, have students stop. Dramatically complain about how the shaking tires you out. Then ask, "What would happen if I gave up shaking the bag? Would I have any pudding to eat?" Lead children to conclude that finishing the task is the best option. Direct them to continue shaking until the pudding is mixed. Then snip a corner from each bag and have them slurp this enjoyable treat!

Suzanne Moore

Tortoise or Hare?

Making real-life connections, answering questions about a story

In advance, cut out a copy of the cards on page 242 and, on a sheet of chart paper, write the statements shown. Read aloud a traditional version of _The Tortoise and the Hare_. Then read aloud the first statement. Have students decide which character matches the statement. Have a volunteer pick up a corresponding character card and attach it to the chart. Continue with each remaining statement.

Cindy Hoying
Centerville, OH

For extra fun, attach tortoise and hare cards to separate blocks and place them in your block center. Youngsters can re-create the race with the props!

This character wasted time doing other things.

This character fell asleep.

This character did his best.

This character thought for sure he would win.

This character kept trying.

This character was slow but steady.

This character made smart choices.

The character was fast but didn't focus on the race.

Involve Your Mascot!

To encourage youngsters to show perseverance, develop a class theme that you can repeat when the going gets tough. Soon youngsters will be repeating it too! When faced with a tough task, say, "[School and mascot] never give up!" (for example, "Webster Winners never give up!"). Students will develop an understanding of perseverance without even knowing it!

Amy Bruening, Webster Elementary, Yankton, SD

I've Been Working!

Participating in a song

Remind youngsters that learning letter names can be very challenging, but it's important to never give up so they will become terrific readers! Then lead them in singing this song. Consider singing other versions of this song, replacing "letters" with "numbers," "manners," or "rhyming."

(sung to the tune of "I've Been Working on the Railroad")

I've been working on my letters,
Working the whole day through.
I've been working on my letters.
It is very hard to do!
Never, ever will I give up!
Work, work, work the day through.
I will surely learn my letters.
That is what I'll do!

Tortoise and Hare Cards

Use with "Tortoise or Hare?" on page 241.

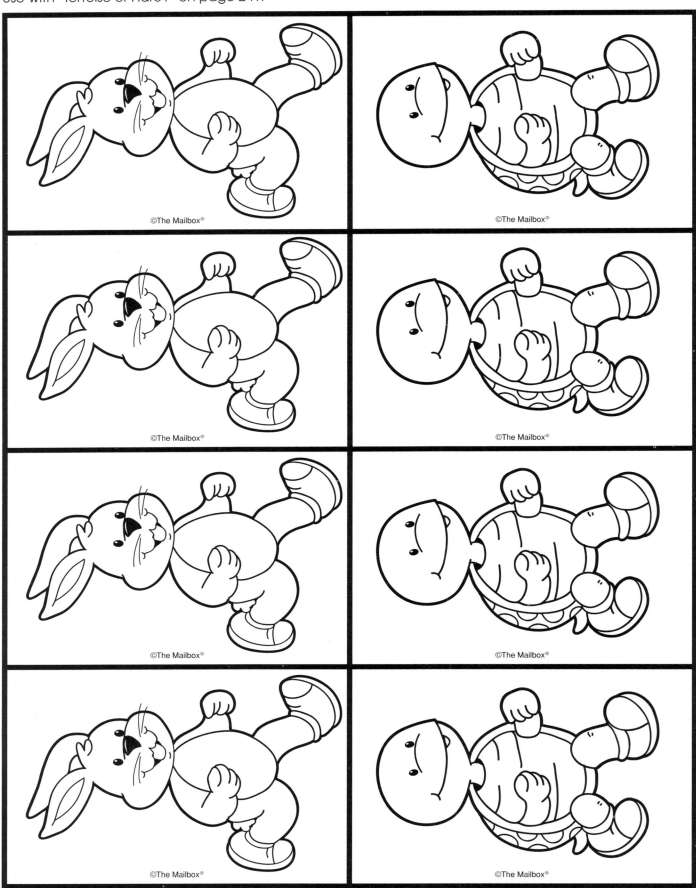

©The Mailbox®

©The Mailbox®

©The Mailbox®

©The Mailbox®

©The Mailbox®

©The Mailbox®

©The Mailbox®

©The Mailbox®

Please Be Polite

Spotlight polite words with activities that will have your little ones saying "Thank you!"

Smart Kids Say...

Cut out a copy of the cards on page 245 and place them in a gift bag. Have a child choose one of the cards from the bag. Read the card aloud and encourage youngsters to answer the question, leading them to use polite words in their answers. Next, prompt students to recite the rhyme shown. Repeat the process with each remaining card.

I am smart,
And smart kids say,
"Thank you, please, excuse me"
Every day!

Cindy Hoying
Centerville, OH

You accidentally bump into a child when you're playing. What should you say?

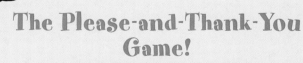

The Please-and-Thank-You Game!

Developing gross-motor skills

Give Duck, Duck, Goose a politeness spin with this whole-group game! Have little ones sit in a circle. Choose a youngster and have him walk around the circle. After a few moments, have him tap a classmate on the shoulder and say, "Will you please [jump] with me?" Prompt the chosen child to say, "Yes, thank you!" Have the students jump together as they count to five. Then have the youngsters switch places. Encourage the new child to begin another round. After several rounds, announce a new gross-motor movement to replace jumping!

Words So Right!

Participating in a song

Guide little ones in singing this toe-tapping song. Then encourage youngsters to share when they might use these polite phrases.

(sung to the tune of "Are You Sleeping?")

[_Please_ and _thank you_],
[_Please_ and _thank you_],
Words so right—so polite!
Be kind to each other.
Be kind to each other.
Words so right—so polite.

Continue with the following: _Please excuse me, I'm so sorry, You are welcome, May I please?_

Cindy Hoying
Centerville, OH

P Is for _Polite_

Identifying letters

Place a variety of letter cards in a basket, including several _P_s. Seat little ones in a circle and give a child the basket. Then play music and have youngsters pass the basket around the circle. Stop the music and encourage the child with the basket to choose a card and hold it up. Help students identify the letter. If it's a letter _P_, prompt the child with the card to recall a polite word or phrase, such as _please_, _excuse me_, or _thank you_.

Cindy Hoying

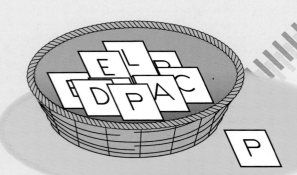

Good Morning!

Speaking

It's often difficult to get little ones to respond when an adult tells them "good morning." Remind youngsters to respond with equally polite words with this prop! Make a large, smiling sun stick puppet. Explain to students that when they arrive in the morning, you'll be carrying your sun puppet. When you say "good morning" to them, they'll see you smile as wide as the sun when they say "good morning" in return. After your youngsters and you greet each other the next morning, praise them for being so kind and polite!

A child can't reach a block in the block center. How should he ask another child for the block?

©The Mailbox®

You ask if you can have a turn playing on a swing. Your friend says, "Yes," and gets off the swing. What should you say in return?

©The Mailbox®

A classmate sneezes. What should he do? What should he say?

©The Mailbox®

You accidentally bump into a child when you're playing. What should you say?

©The Mailbox®

Your teacher says, "Good morning!" What should you say in return?

©The Mailbox®

You are playing with a friend and his mom gives you a cookie. What should you say?

©The Mailbox®

Caring Kids!

Youngsters who are caring are kind, helpful, and forgiving. Encourage these traits with simple and fun activities!

Help a friend zip a jacket.

Share your toys.

Say, "I'm sorry" if you bump into someone.

Nice Dice

Participating in a group game

Cut out the cards on page 247 and then attach each one to a different side of a foam die (or square box). Each morning for several days, have a child roll the die. Then read the caring card that is faceup. Explain that this is the caring reminder for the day. Then discuss its meaning and give examples or act out how children could go about the task. Have students keep this goal in mind as they go throughout their school day.

Betty Silkunas, Fernandina Beach, FL

When You're Caring

Participating in a song

Help youngsters understand the traits of a caring person with this bouncy song!

(sung to the tune of "If You're Happy and You Know It")

When you're caring and you know it, [you are kind].
When you're caring and you know it, [you are kind].
When you're caring and you know it,
Then your words and actions show it.
When you're caring and you know it, [you are kind].

Continue with the following: you will help, you forgive

Doria Owen, William Paca Old Post Road Elementary, Abingdon, MD

Friendly Words

Building vocabulary

Involve your youngsters in the establishment of a caring classroom climate by having them brainstorm a list of friendly words to use every day. Before beginning, help them understand the difference between friendly and unfriendly words. Talk about how some words make people feel good or happy when people say them. Other words have the opposite effect. Write the brainstormed words on construction paper cards and display them in a pocket chart. Use these words in the chant below.

Friendly words, friendly words,
Use them every day.
Friendly words, friendly words
Feel so good to say.
[Chant your list of brainstormed words.]

kind

happy

friendly

nice

helpful

Play with someone new.

©The Mailbox®

Say, "I'm sorry" if you bump into someone.

©The Mailbox®

Help a friend zip a jacket.

©The Mailbox®

Use kind words when we're getting in line.

©The Mailbox®

Share your toys.

©The Mailbox®

Compliment a friend.

©The Mailbox®

Think Before You Act!

Read aloud a favorite version of *Chicken Little* (or *Henny Penny*) to help students learn that they should gather the facts before they react. Then engage youngsters in this selection of activities that will guide them in learning self-control.

Plop!

After reading aloud the story, ask youngsters to name things Chicken Little could have done to show self-control when the acorn hit his head, such as finding out what hit him and taking a deep breath to calm down. Help students generate several strategies to use when upset and record them on an oversize acorn cutout. Then invite youngsters, in turn, to pretend to be Chicken Little. As each child walks along, drop a large brown pom-pom (acorn) on her head and have her demonstrate one of the strategies listed.

Stop and Think!

Chicken Little uses self-control in this engaging rhyme! Have each child make a stick puppet that shows the main character in the version of the story read to your students (see page 250 for patterns). Read aloud the poem shown, encouraging youngsters to chant the last line of each stanza with you while holding their puppets in the air.

Chicken Little felt something fall from the sky.
It hit his head! He wanted to cry!
Stop and think, Chicken Little!

Rather than guessing what hit his head,
He stopped to look around instead.
Stop and think, Chicken Little!

He looked on the ground, and what he saw
Was an acorn nearby! The sky didn't fall!
Stop and think, Chicken Little!

Chicken Little moved from under the tree
So he wouldn't get hit again, you see.
Stop and think, Chicken Little!

In Control

This idea encourages the whole class to practice self-control! Make a simple display similar to the one shown (see page 250 for character patterns). Then discuss with youngsters scenarios that sometimes cause self-control issues, such as sharing and turn taking. Ask students to name ways to show self-control in each situation. Throughout the week when self-control is shown, record student behavior on separate acorn cutouts. Then invite each child to attach his acorn to the display.

One, Two, Think It Through!

The story might have turned out differently if Chicken Little had known this nifty chant! Teach your little ones the chant shown to help them keep their cool and think things through!

One, two, think it through.
Three, four, think some more.
Five, six, the clock ticks.
Seven, eight, still I wait.
Nine, ten, now I'm ready again!

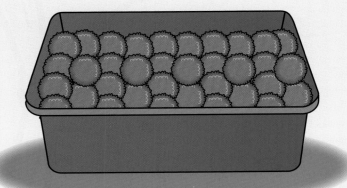

Acorn Squeeze

Remind little ones to calm down and think before they act with an acorn-themed sensory area. Gather brown pom-poms (acorns) and place them in a small tub. When a child needs to calm down and think, encourage her to visit the area and squeeze and squish the acorns. If desired, place a muffin tin in the area as well and the child can count the acorns as she places them in the tin. Remind her to breathe deeply and slowly as she works. When she is feeling more calm, she can rejoin her classmates.

Chicken Little and Henny Penny Patterns
Use with "Stop and Think!" on page 248 and "In Control" on page 249.

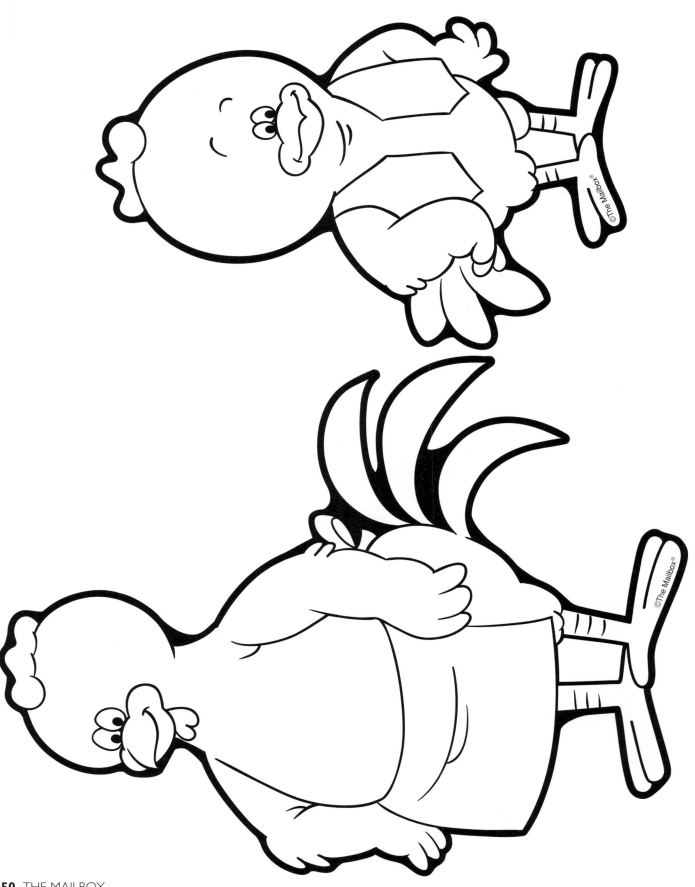

MANAGING YOUR CLASSROOM

Ladybugs on a Leaf

Try this idea to **help little ones who have a difficult time coming inside** after outdoor play! Cut out a class supply of the ladybugs on page 252 and place the hook side of a piece of Velcro fastener on each one. Post a supersize leaf cutout on your wall and attach the loop side of the Velcro fasteners to the leaf. When it's time to line up to come inside, give each child a ladybug and say, "It's time to put your ladybug on your leaf!" Students will be eager to come in and attach their ladybugs!

Ammie Munnik, Wood County Head Start
Vesper, WI

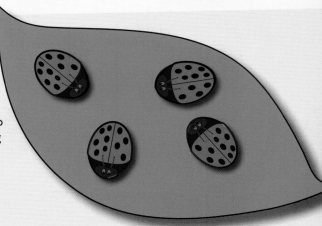

A Classroom Tree

Appreciate student accomplishments with a star tree! Attach a large leafless tree cutout to your wall. Die-cut a variety of colorful stars. When a child has an accomplishment—anything from learning her colors to not hitting during centers—write it on a star and tell the child how proud you are of her. Then have her attach the star to the tree.

Deborah J. Ryan, Newberg, OR

Cleanup Mystery Item

Add a fun twist to your cleanup time with this game! Before students clean up, survey the room. Then write on a sticky note the name of one item that needs to be picked up and thrown away. Have little ones pick up items and place them at their seats. Then reveal the item and see who picked it up. Add a cute sticker to the note and give it to the child to take home. Then walk the trash can around so students can throw away their items.

Emily Porter, Scott County Schools
Georgetown, KY

Class.

Attention Grabber!

To **get students' attention in a fun way**, say "class" in different voices, such as a baby voice, a monster voice, a big voice, and a ghost voice. After each one, the children repeat the word with the same inflection. Fun!

Kelly Tincher, Saint Edmond School
Fort Dodge, IA

Ladybug Patterns

Use with "Ladybugs on a Leaf" on page 251.

©The Mailbox®

THEMATIC UNITS

Splish, Splash! An Ocean-Themed Welcome!

Welcome little ones to preschool with displays and activities that are sure to make a splash!

Castles in the Sand

Attendance display

Take attendance with this adorable display! Cut out a class supply of the sand castle on page 256. Then personalize a castle for each child and laminate the castles for durability. To take attendance, place the castles on a tabletop or on the floor in your circle time area. A child finds his sand castle and then pushes it into your sand table (or a tub full of sand) so it's standing up. The remaining sand castles tell you who isn't present for the day. Too cute!

Who Is the Star?

Daily helper chart

Instead of having a variety of classroom job titles to keep track of, just have one star student complete the jobs for the day! Personalize a sea star cutout for each child. (See page 256 for a pattern.) Then attach the cutouts to a wall around a treasure chest cutout. Each day, attach a different sea star to the treasure chest. For extra fun, allow the star child to wear treasure, such as some fun bangle bracelets, for the day. This child can be the line leader, water classroom plants, pass out special treats, and help with any other special jobs for the day.

No room for a display? Keep the sea stars in an ocean-themed gift bag. Then just pull out a cutout each day!

Ocean Collage
Arts and crafts

For this simple craft project, collect a variety of ocean-themed cutouts, green paper shreds (seaweed), and brown hole-punch dots and gold glitter (sand). Place a 9" x 13" piece of Con-Tact covering sticky-side up on a table. Then have a child press the cutouts and shreds on the surface. Next, prompt her to sprinkle dots and glitter as well. Finally, press a 9" x 13" sheet of blue construction paper onto the Con-Tact covering. Then flip the project over to reveal an ocean masterpiece!

Ashley Young
Lincoln Lab Children's Center
Lexington, MA

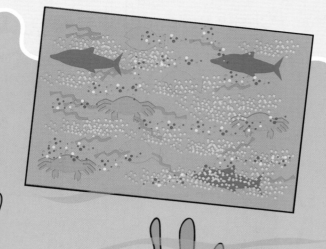

Fishing for Names
Getting-acquainted activity

Youngsters get to know each other better with this twist on a traditional fishing game! Cut out several copies of the ocean critters on page 257. Personalize and attach a paper clip to each cutout. Make a fishing pole by tying a magnet to a length of yarn and tying the other end to a ruler or dowel. Scatter the cutouts in the middle of your group-time area. Then have a child use the pole to "catch" a cutout. Read aloud the name on the cutout and encourage everyone to say hello to that child. Then give her the pole and have her fish for a different cutout.

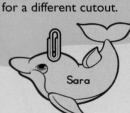

Let's Swim!
Song

Cut out a copy of the ocean critters on page 257. Attach a sheet of blue paper to your wall. Then attach the dolphin to the wall and lead students in singing the song shown as they pretend to swim like a dolphin. Repeat the process for each remaining critter!

(sung to the tune of "My Bonnie Lies Over the Ocean")

A [dolphin] swims out in the ocean,
And that is where [dolphins] should be.
Oh, how I would love to go with it.
Together—a [dolphin] and me!
Swimming, swimming
Together—a [dolphin] and me, and me!
Swimming, swimming
Together—a [dolphin] and me!

Cindy Hoying
Centerville, OH

Sand Castle Pattern
Use with "Castles in the Sand" on page 254.

©The Mailbox®

Sea Star Pattern
Use with "Who Is the Star?" on page 254.

©The Mailbox®

Ocean Critter Patterns
Use with "Fishing for Names"
and "Let's Swim!" on page 255.

Welcome-to-School Centers

This selection of centers is perfect for the beginning of the school year. Why? They're easy to prepare and will keep little fingers and minds engaged!

So Shiny!

Sand Table

Your little ones will love searching for shiny sequins! Place colorful sequins in your sand table and provide small containers. Encourage youngsters to pick the sequins from the sand and place them in a container. For a more challenging center, place the sequins in a tub full of rainbow-colored rice! *Five senses: sight, touch*

Deborah J. Ryan, Newberg, OR

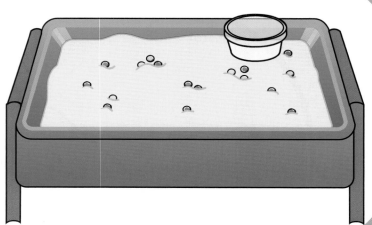

Wonderful Wallets

Dramatic-Play Area

Gather old empty wallets and fill them with a variety of old gift cards and pretend money. (If you don't have any old wallets, thrift stores are excellent sources.) Place the wallets at a center and encourage students to role-play. Youngsters will enjoy pretending to pay for things just like grown-ups do! *Role playing*

Megan Taylor, Rowlett, TX

Big Red Apple!

Fine-Motor Area

Provide a supersize red apple cutout, glue sticks, scissors, and magazines. Attach the apple to a table top. Students visit the center, rip or cut pictures of red items from the magazines, and then glue them to the apple. Have students continue until the entire apple is covered. Then display it in the classroom! *Developing fine-motor skills, matching colors, recognizing colors*

Megan Taylor
Rowlett, TX

Block Soup

Block Center

Add this unique play option to your block center! Place large plastic mixing bowls and mixing spoons at your block center. A child pretends to be a chef as he places blocks in a mixing bowl to make delicious soup or stew! Then he uses a mixing spoon to stir his concoction. What fun! *Role playing*

If desired, provide cookbooks for youngsters to look through. They'll enjoy pretending to create the recipes they see, and you'll love that they're developing print awareness!

Navigating My Name

Writing Center

For each child, program a large sheet of construction paper with her name. Provide small toy vehicles, large craft feathers, chopsticks, pipe cleaners, and other manipulatives. Place the manipulatives near shallow containers of paint. A child dips a manipulative in the paint and then drags it over each letter in her name. She repeats the process with different manipulatives. *Forming letters*

Tricia Kylene Brown, Bowling Green, KY

Party Time!

Art Center

Get curling ribbon, star stickers, and birthday-themed wrapping paper scraps and place them at your art center. Also, write each child's name and birthdate on separate sheets of construction paper. Give a visiting child her paper and read aloud her name and birthdate while you follow the words with your finger. Next, have the child decorate the paper with ribbon, stickers, and wrapping paper. *Reinforcing personal information*

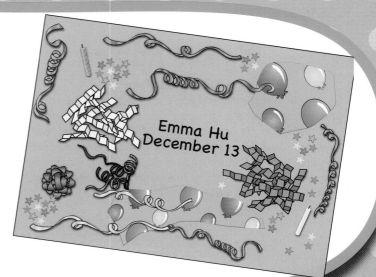

Subtle Sounds

Sensory Center

Youngsters make subtle sounds with every item at this center! Provide items such as a ring of keys, Velcro fasteners, Bubble Wrap cushioning material, a water bottle partially filled with water, a plastic egg with rice or beans inside (secure the egg with tape), and retractable pens. Place the items at the center. A youngster visits the center and uses the various props to make noise. *Investigating the sense of hearing*

Megan Taylor
Rowlett, TX

Wormy Apples

Math Center

At this center, youngsters will wiggle on over to match each little worm with an apple! Make copies of page 261. Color and cut out the patterns. Place the apples and worms at a center. Have each child use one-to-one correspondence to match one worm to each apple. *One-to-one correspondence*

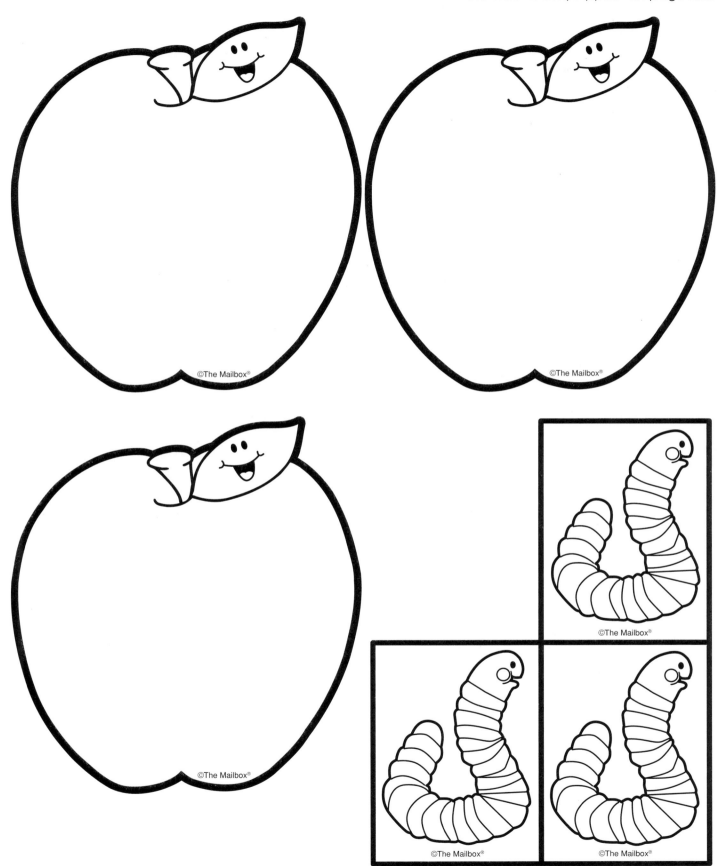

©The Mailbox®

©The Mailbox®

©The Mailbox®

©The Mailbox®

©The Mailbox®

©The Mailbox®

City and Country

What can you see in the city? What can you see in the country? Little ones learn with this selection of activities that encourage youngsters to compare and contrast!

ideas contributed by Cindy Hoying
Centerville, OH

Tall or Wide?
Using descriptive words

Guide little ones in singing this action song that also provides a great stretching opportunity!

(sung to the tune of "The Farmer in the Dell")

Tall buildings way up high,   *Stretch with arms raised.*
Tall buildings way up high,
Oh my! They reach the sky!
Tall buildings way up high.

A land that's far and wide,   *Stretch with arms outward.*
A land that's far and wide,
See crops grow side by side.
A land that's far and wide.

Silo Five Frame
Using the word less, identifying numbers

Color and cut out a copy of the silo pattern on page 264 and place it at a center along with pieces of yellow yarn (hay). Gather number cards from 1 to 5 and arrange them facedown. Gather two youngsters at the center and explain that a silo is a tower on a farm that's used to store grain or hay. Then have a child choose a card and help him identify the number. Prompt his partner to count the corresponding pieces of hay and place one in each space on the silo. Help youngsters understand that the number of hay pieces is less than five. Then encourage them to work together to decide how many more pieces are needed to make five. Finally, have them remove the hay and then play again.

Country Night, City Night
Comparing locations, fine-motor skills

To make this simple artwork, fold a sheet of dark blue or purple paper in half. On one side of the folded paper, draw a hill with a black crayon. Then glue a small black house shape on the hill. Glue two squares of yellow tissue paper (windows) to the house. Then attach star stickers to the sky. On the opposite half of the paper, glue black construction paper skyscrapers. Use a white crayon to make dots (windows) on the skyscrapers. Then rub the side of the crayon on the page to make a soft glow.

So Many Sounds
Identifying characteristics of city and country

Sing this song with your youngsters. After each verse, ask whether the sound mentioned might be heard in the country or in the city.

(sung to the tune of "This Old Man")

Here a sound,
There a sound,
Tell me where this sound is found.
Hear [a moo, moo, moo
And cock-a-doodle-doo!]
Tell me where this sound is found.

Continue with the following:
a beep, beep, beep. The cars and buses creep!
a cluck, cluck, cluck. I hear the farmer's truck.
a talk, talk, talk of people as they walk.
an owl go "Whoooo!" and crickets chirping too.

Find It, Stick It!
Recognizing letters, forming letters

Get a copy of *Alphabet City* by Stephen T. Johnson. This picture book is filled with paintings that depict urban life. Each painting also conceals a letter of the alphabet! Guide youngsters through the book. For each page, have a student point out the letter; then have students "draw" the letter in the air with their fingers. Next, place the book at a center along with sticky notes and pencils or crayons. A student looks at a page and finds the letter. Then she writes the letter on a sticky note and sticks it to the page. She continues for several pages.

ALPHABET CITY

Stephen T. Johnson

See page 265 for a **reproducible** on **classification!**

Silo Pattern

Use with "Silo Five Frame" on page 262.

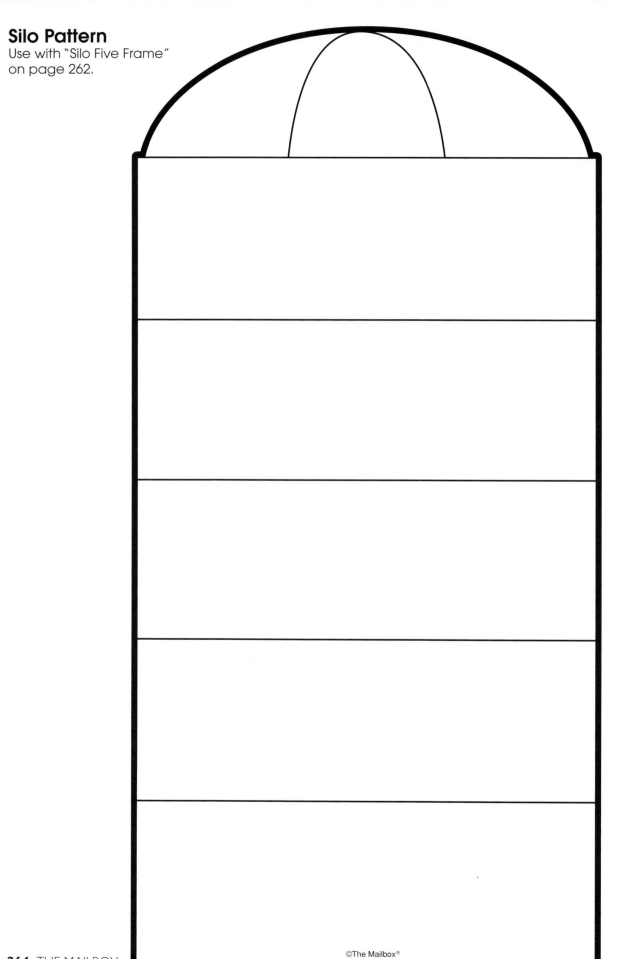

One Doesn't Belong

Put an X on the one that is different in each row.
Color the ones that are alike.

Home, Sweet Home!

Investigate animal homes with this creative and fun selection of ideas!

ideas contributed by Roxanne LaBell Dearman
NC Intervention for the Deaf and Hard of Hearing, Charlotte, NC

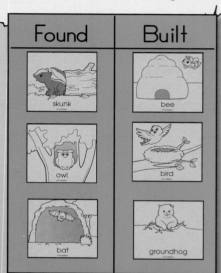

Found	Built
skunk	bee
owl	bird
bat	groundhog

Found or Built?
Organizing data

Some animal homes are found by their occupants and others are built. Help little ones create a chart showing the two with this idea! Cut out a copy of the animal cards on page 268 and place them in a bag. Prepare a chart similar to the one shown. To begin, have a child choose a card from the bag. Read the card to the class. Then have the class decide if the animal built something or if it just found its home. Then have a youngster attach the card to the appropriate side of the chart. Continue with each remaining card.

Rocks, Sticks, and Mud
Participating in a song

Show little ones a picture of a beaver lodge. Explain that beavers build lodges from rocks, sticks, and mud. Then lead them in singing this song. After several rounds, consider completing the "Busy Beavers" activity on page 267.

(sung to the tune of "If You're Happy and You Know It")

See the beaver build its home with some [rocks].
See the beaver build its home with some [rocks].
See the beaver work away in the nighttime, not the day.
See the beaver build its home with some [rocks].

Continue with the following: *sticks, mud*

Cindy Hoying
Centerville, OH

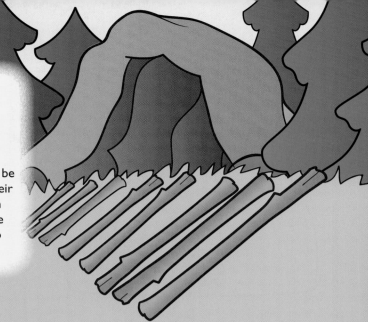

Busy Beavers
Sequencing by length

Gather two sticks for each child, making sure that the sticks are various lengths. Then hide the sticks around the room. After discussing that beavers build dams and lodges with sticks, rocks, and mud, invite little ones to pretend to be beavers and each find two sticks. Prompt them to place their sticks in the middle of the circle time area. Then help them arrange the sticks from shortest to longest. Later, place the sticks at your science center so youngsters can pretend to build beaver lodges.

Cozy Caves
Observing, using the senses

Why would a cave be a good place to live? Youngsters find out with this simple activity! In advance, drape heavy material, such as a sleeping bag, over a small table so it resembles a cave. Leave a small opening to the cave. Then place a blowing fan nearby. Ask little ones to share what they know about caves and about animals that might live in caves. Explain that caves can be homes to animals such as bats, bears, foxes, and wolves. Invite students to visit the cave and notice that it is very windy outside the cave. Ask, "Can you feel the wind very much when you're inside the cave?" Also ask students if they think animals would feel rain inside the cave. Help them conclude that caves shelter animals from the weather and help keep them safe.

In a Tree?
Classifying, fine-motor skills

Living in a tree sounds like a lot of fun! On the board, write the names of several animals, including several tree dwellers. Be sure to space out the names. Read aloud one of the names; then have students decide if the animal lives in a tree. If it does, have a child draw around the name a shape that looks like tree foliage. Continue with each name. Then give each child a copy of page 269. Have her draw her favorite tree dweller on the tree and write the name in the space provided.

bee
©The Mailbox®

bird
©The Mailbox®

skunk
©The Mailbox®

groundhog
©The Mailbox®

owl
©The Mailbox®

bat
©The Mailbox®

This is a _____.

It lives in a tree.

"Whoooo" Loves Owls?

Your little ones will love this selection of activities about these fascinating birds!

Owl Vision

Exploring the senses of touch and sight, investigating living things, fine-motor skills

Youngsters get an idea of what owls eat with this center search! Put small-animal bedding in your empty sand table. If desired, add leaves, sticks, and pinecones so the bedding resembles a forest floor. Then hide toy mice and snakes in the bedding. (For an easy alternative, use gray pom-poms as mice and lengths of green yarn as snakes.) Also provide a container (owl nest) and a magnifying glass. A youngster at the center uses his owl eyes (magnifying glass) to find the snakes and mice. Then he uses his talons (pincer grasp) to pick up the creatures and place them in the nest. That looks like a midnight snack!

Janet Boyce
Hinojosa Early Childhood and Pre-Kindergarten Center
Houston, TX

Owls in the Tree

Counting, making a set

Little ones will love to be owls for this cute song! Designate an area as a treetop. (For extra fun, cut a green shape from bulletin board paper so it resembles a tree and place it on your floor.) Have a child pretend to be an owl, "fly" to the tree, and sit down. Lead students in singing the song shown. Then prompt the little owl to hoot enthusiastically. Repeat the song several times, adding more owls to the tree and tweaking the lyrics as needed.

(sung to the tune of the chorus of "Skip to My Lou")

[One] owl sitting in the tree,
[One] owl sitting in the tree,
[One] owl sitting in the tree,
It hoots, hoots, hoots at me!

Cindy Hoying
Centerville, OH

Wise Owl

Following oral directions

Give youngsters' listening skills a workout with this easy-to-prepare activity! Gather a small group of students and give each child a copy of page 274. Then explain to youngsters that the wise old owl has some directions it wants to see if they can follow. Next, read aloud each direction below, pausing to allow students time to complete the task. Observe as they work and jot down any notes needed for assessment. Depending on your students' attention span, you may want to use only a few of the directions.

Directions:
1. Color the sun.
2. Find the small circle. Color it blue.
3. Cross out the leaf.
4. Color the butterfly.
5. Draw dots on the balloon.
6. Draw a smiley face on the pumpkin.
7. Color the squirrel brown.
8. Cross out the rectangle.
9. Find the empty box at the bottom of the page. Draw raindrops.

Fun Fact!
Did you know that owls can turn their heads as much as 270 degrees? Show your little ones an online video of this ability! (A search for "owl turning head" will give you several options.) Then have youngsters compare this to their own flexibility. Fun!

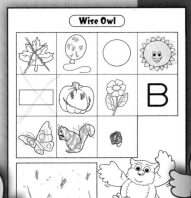

Wise Owl

Sound Asleep

Developing fine-motor skills

To make the owl bodies, trim a large and small paper plate as shown. Use a thick brown crayon without a wrapper to rub both sides of each plate. Then draw closed eyes and a beak on each owl. Next, fringe-cut the ridged areas (wings) of each owl body. Fold the wings of each owl so they overlap in front of the owl's face. Finally, stand the owls so the little one is inside the big one's protective wings.

Janet Boyce
Cokato, MN

Owl Babies

Written by Martin Waddell
Illustrated by Patrick Benson

When three baby owls awaken and find that their mother isn't in the nest, they worry and wonder where she is. Much excited flapping greets her when she returns!

ideas contributed by Cindy Hoying
Centerville, OH

Pass the Owl

Speaking to answer questions about a story, recalling story events

Read aloud *Owl Babies* by Martin Waddell. Then have students sit in a circle. Give a large white pom-pom (Bill, the owlet) to a child. Ask him one of the questions shown. After he answers, have him pass Bill to a classmate. Continue with a different question.

How many baby owls are in the story?
What are their names?
Why are they worried?
Are they happy to see their mother? How do you know?
What is your favorite part of the story?
Have you ever been afraid of something? What was it?
What can you do to make yourself feel better when you're afraid?
Have you ever missed someone you love?

Here Comes Mom!

Counting

Have little ones complete this number line activity that reunites the mother owl and her babies! Write a number line from 1–10 on a strip of brown paper (branch). Give the number line to a child and have her place one large brown pom-pom (mother owl) near the number one and three small white pom-poms (owlets) near the number ten. Next, have her roll a die and count the dots. Then have her move the mother owl that many spaces toward her babies. Continue rolling until she reaches her babies. (It's okay if the final roll takes her beyond the range of the number line.) **For a more difficult activity,** consider using a number line from 1 to 20.

Let's Be Owls!

Youngsters use their imaginations to investigate the anatomy of these interesting birds!

Materials:
owl photos (An Internet image search will turn up many options.)

STEP 1

Ask youngsters to share what they know about owls. Then show them several photos of owls and have them discuss what they see. Say, "Let's pretend to be owls." Explain that owls have eyes that face forward like ours do. (Other birds have eyes on the sides of their heads.) Owls have very large eyes. Have students make circles with their hands and put them up to their eyes. Then prompt them to use their "giant owl eyes" to scan the room for "food," like mice, insects, or snakes. Encourage them to "catch" some pretend food.

STEP 2

Explain that some owls have very good hearing. This is important so they can hear creatures they want to catch and eat. Have students place their hands alongside their heads and pretend to listen for rustling creatures.

STEP 3

Ask students how owls get from place to place. (They fly!) Explain that owls have special feathers, which let them fly quietly. Ask, "Why would owls need to fly quietly?" Lead youngsters to understand that flying quietly helps owls sneak up on their prey. Next, have students "fly" around the room as quietly as possible.

STEP 4

Finally, explain that owls have talons on the ends of their toes. Talons are sharp claws that help them perch on branches and also catch small animals. Have your little owls stand and pretend to balance on a tree branch by digging in their "talons."

What Next?

Set up a center to encourage owl-related dramatic play. Provide a balance beam or a length of brown paper for a branch. Drape a blanket over a table, leaving a small opening, so little owls can pretend that it's an owl nest in the hole of a tree. Provide plastic mice and snakes for "food." Then invite students to the center!

Wise Owl

Note to the teacher: Use with "Wise Owl" on page 271.

©The Mailbox®

HAPPY Thanksgiving Day!

Celebrate family time and fabulous food with a selection of activities on this thankful holiday!

ideas contributed by Cindy Hoying, Centerville, OH

Where's the Mayflower?
Counting

For this math activity, attach a length of wavy blue bulletin board border (ocean waves) to a wall. At the end of the border, attach a brown sheet of paper to represent land. Color and cut out a copy of the *Mayflower* pattern on page 278 and place removable adhesive on the back. Gather number cards and then slip several cards labeled with raindrops in the stack. Place the cards facedown. To begin, lead students in singing the song. Have a child choose a card and move the *Mayflower* forward, counting the waves to equal the number on her card. Continue in the same way, singing the song before each move. If the child selects a raindrop card, have students pat the floor to make rain sounds and move the *Mayflower* back one space. Prompt students to give a cheer when the *Mayflower* finally reaches land.

(*sung to the tune of "My Bonnie Lies Over the Ocean"*)
The *Mayflower* sailed on the ocean.
The water's the bluest you'll see.
The *Mayflower* sailed on the ocean.
Oh, where can that *Mayflower* be?

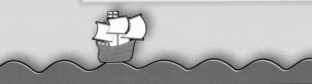

Pumpkin Pie Process Art
Expressing oneself through art, fine-motor skills

The setup for this project is as easy as pie! Cut small wedge shapes (pumpkin pie slices) from craft foam. Then use duct tape (or another sturdy tape) to make a handle on each slice. Place the slices near very shallow containers of orange paint. A child holds the handle and presses the slice in the paint. Then he makes pumpkin pie slice prints on a sheet of paper.

Mashed Potato Pile
Measurement, comparing size

Gather cotton balls (mashed potatoes), disposable bowls, and strips of tagboard in different lengths. Place the items at a center. A child chooses a strip and then piles mashed potatoes in a bowl until it reaches the height of the strip. He repeats the process with a second strip. Then he compares the heights of the bowls of mashed potatoes. He empties the bowls and repeats the activity again with two different strips.

Say "Thank You"!
Exploring the meaning of a holiday

Spotlight the meaning of Thanksgiving Day with a song that encourages youngsters to be thankful!

(sung to the tune of "The Farmer in the Dell")

It's time to say "thank you"!
It's time to say "thank you"!
For [friends and family] too,
It's time to say "thank you"!

Continue with the following: *food and shelter, sun and raindrops, love and kindness, pie and turkey, smiles and laughter*

Pumpkin Pie Man
Beginning sound /p/

Color and cut out a copy of the pumpkin pie man pattern on page 278. Then attach it to a craft stick to make a puppet. Also cut out a copy of the food picture cards on page 279. Place the cards in a pocket chart. To begin, hold up the puppet and lead students in reciting the rhyme shown. Give the puppet to a child and have him approach the pocket chart. Encourage him to name one of the pictures that begins with /p/ and have him pretend the pumpkin pie man is gobbling up that food. Then have him give the puppet to a classmate. Recite the rhyme again and continue in the same way. After all the picture names that begin with /p/ have been identified, have students point out the names that do not begin with /p/.

Gobble, gobble, pumpkin pie—
How many /p/ foods do you spy?

Guests at the Feast!
Developing gross-motor skills

Little ones are sure to ask for repeated performances of this action song! Lead youngsters in singing the song and performing the movements. If desired, prompt students to come up with more verses.

(sung to the tune of "The Wheels on the Bus")

The guests at the feast [sit down in chairs], *Pantomime sitting and standing.*
[Down in chairs, down in chairs].
The guests at the feast [sit down in chairs]
On Thanksgiving Day.

Continue with the following:

all pass the food	*Pretend to pass a dish from left to right.*
go chomp, chomp, chomp	*Pretend to feed self.*
go talk, talk, talk	*Move hands as if they were mouths.*
clean up the plates	*Rub pretend plate in a circular motion.*
say, "Thanks so much"	*Make the American Sign Language sign (see reference).*
go out the door	*Walk in place.*

Set the Table
Working with a five frame, counting to answer "How many more?"

This five-frame activity is big on Thanksgiving Day fun! Use masking tape to make a supersize five frame on a tabletop. (Make sure the sections in the five frame will hold paper plates.) Gather five paper plates. Have students count the spaces in the five frame. Then give students an oral problem, such as "Grandma, Grandpa, and Sarah are having Thanksgiving Day dinner. How many plates will they need for the table?" Have students determine that three plates are needed. Encourage a child to place three plates on the five frame. Then ask, "How many more plates are needed to fill up the table?" After youngsters determine that two more plates are needed, remove the plates and challenge them with a new problem!

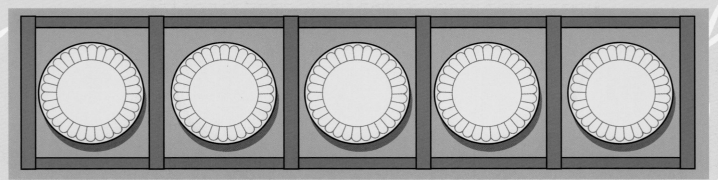

Mayflower Pattern

Use with "Where's the *Mayflower*?" on page 275.

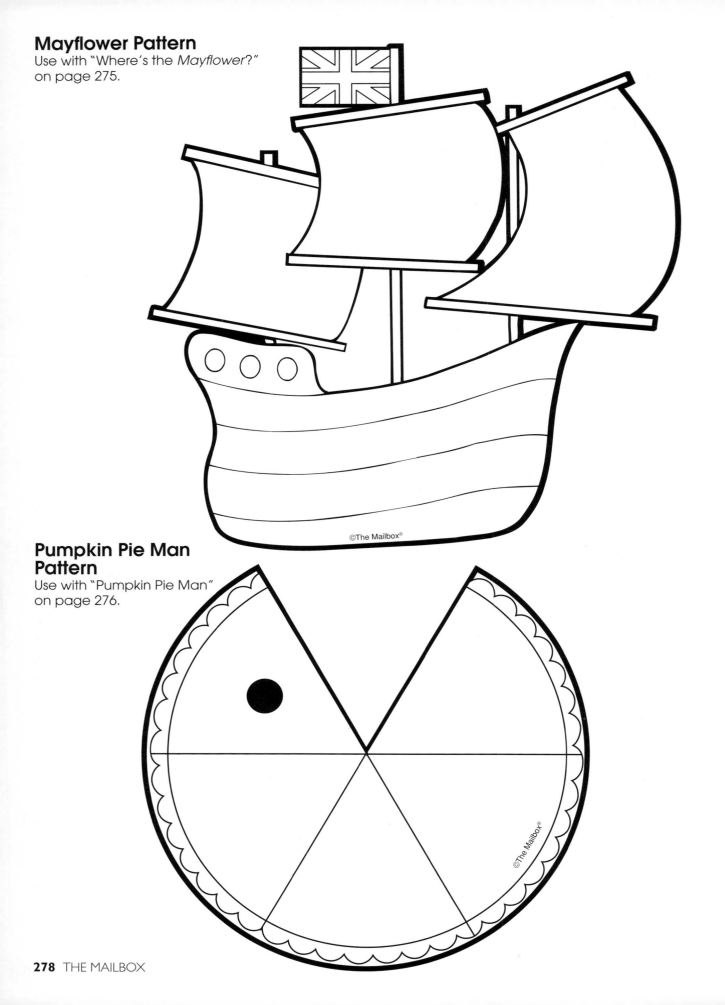

©The Mailbox®

Pumpkin Pie Man Pattern

Use with "Pumpkin Pie Man" on page 276.

©The Mailbox®

©The Mailbox®

©The Mailbox®

©The Mailbox®

©The Mailbox®

©The Mailbox®

©The Mailbox®

©The Mailbox®

©The Mailbox®

©The Mailbox®

Time to Hide!

Wonder Where do turkeys hide on Thanksgiving Day?

Draw

Tell

©The Mailbox®

Note to the teacher: Give a copy of this page to a child. Encourage him to draw to answer the question. Then have him explain his drawing. Write his words at the bottom of the page.

Holiday Lights

Candles, houses, and trees are all lit up for December holidays! Spotlight this lovely illumination with an assortment of vibrant ideas.

Count the Candles

Counting syllables

Wrap an empty oatmeal canister with colorful paper (or gift wrap) so it resembles a large candle. Gather three battery powered tea lights, turn them on, and place them next to the candle. Say one of the words below and then have students clap the word. Next, have a child place the appropriate number of flames on the candle to match. Check for accuracy. Then remove the flames and play another round.

Suggested words: *candle, flame, light, holiday, Christmas, Hanukkah, Kwanzaa, bright, lovely, tree, ornament, family, presents*

Tricia Kylene Brown
Bowling Green, KY

Brilliant Trees!

Making sets

This festive project is a terrific assessment tool! In advance, cut out ten green paper triangles (evergreen trees) and ten small brown rectangles (trunks). Write numbers 1 through 10 on a 12" x 18" sheet of construction paper for each child. Gather shallow pans of paint and unsharpened pencils. To begin, have each child glue a tree and trunk above each number on her sheet of paper. Then have her identify the first number, dip the eraser end of a pencil in paint, and count aloud as she makes one print (light) on the appropriate tree. Have her continue with each tree on the page.

Jenna Dunlop
Mason, OH

Light-Up Nose!

Beginning sound /r/

Rudolph the reindeer has one of the most well-known holiday lights of all! For this literacy activity, cut out 12 copies of the Rudolph head pattern on page 283 and gather red pom-pom noses. (For extra fun, use sparkly pom-poms!) Then place the Rudolph heads on the floor and the pom-poms nearby. Say a word. (See the suggested list.) If the word begins with /r/ like *Rudolph* and *reindeer*, prompt students to touch their noses. Then have a child take a pom-pom nose and place it on a Rudolph. Continue until each Rudolph has a nose!

Suggested words: *rabbits, race, right, soup, raccoon, fence, radio, rag, rainbow, cake, raisin, seal, rake, ring, rip, rope*

Christine Vohs, College Church Preschool, Olathe, KS

String the Lights

Identifying colors, continuing a pattern

Youngsters decorate a house with lovely Christmas lights with this whole-group activity! Cut out a house shape from a large sheet of construction paper and add simple details. Then label the sides and roof of the house with circles so they represent a string of lights. Gather pom-poms in two different colors. Use the pom-poms to create an *AB* pattern on the first few circles. Then choose a child to find and place the next pom-pom. Continue in the same way until the house is outlined with patterned lights!

Tricia Kylene Brown, Bowling Green, KY
Cindy Hoying, Centerville, OH

Night Lights

Identifying colors

Get a colorful string of lights and plug them in. Then have a student point to and identify the color of one of the lights. Lead students in singing a verse of the song, substituting the appropriate color in the blank and encouraging youngsters to flick their fingers each time they say, "Blink, blink!" Continue with each remaining light color.

(sung to the tune of "If You're Happy and You Know It")

There's a [red] Christmas light in the night. (Blink, blink!)
There's a [red] Christmas light in the night. (Blink, blink!)
It will shine its light so bright.
It will glow throughout the night.
There's a [red] Christmas light in the night. (Blink, blink!)

Cindy Hoying

Rudolph Head Pattern

Use with "Light-Up Nose!" on page 282.

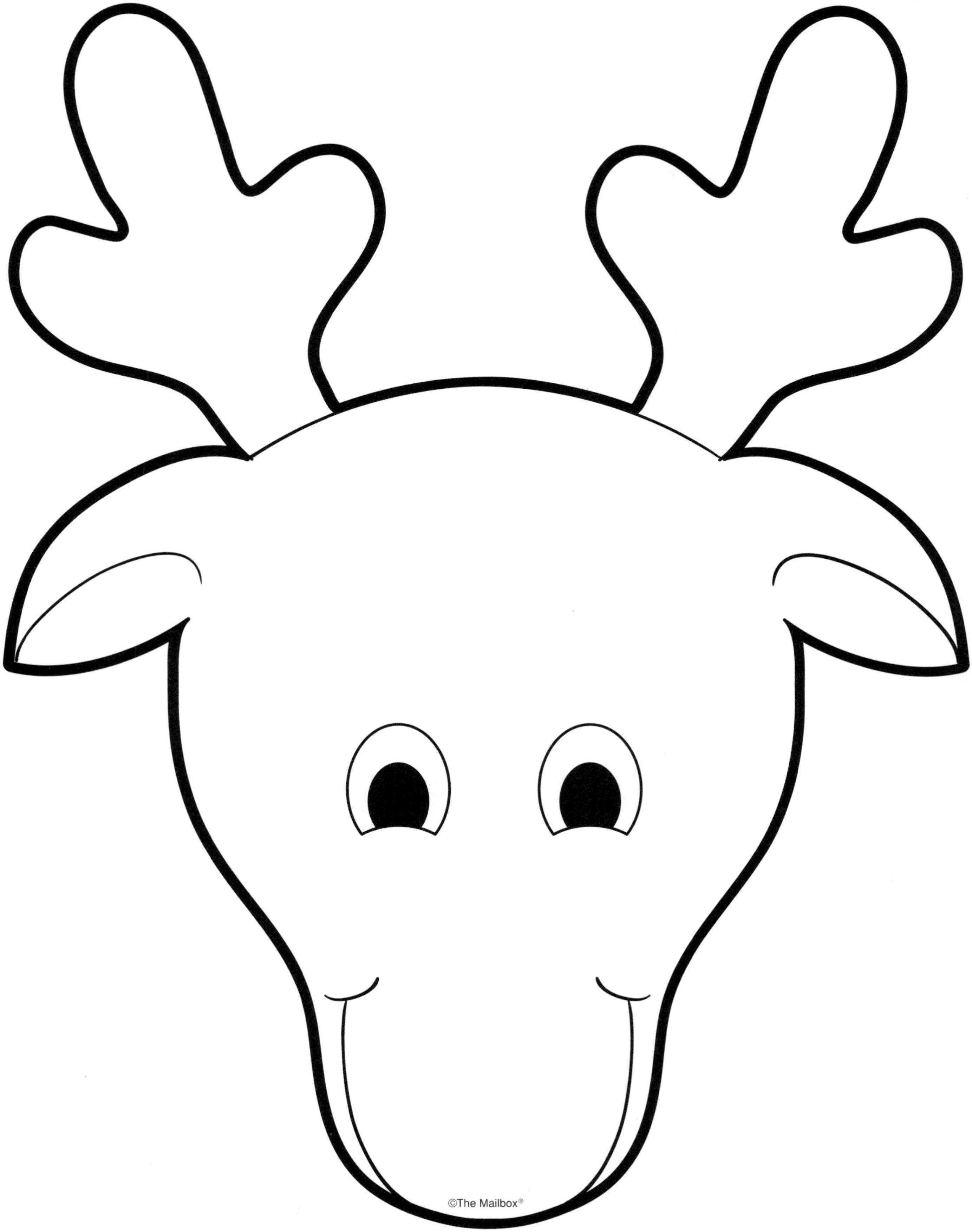

Hooray for Valentine's Day!

Here's a sweet selection of Valentine's Day activities your little ones will love!

Love Leaves

Writing, talking about emotions

This homemade houseplant is a fun February project! In advance, make a supply of heart-shaped leaf cutouts. Have youngsters discuss how they know when they love someone or something. Then have each child write (or dictate) the names of two or three people or things he loves on separate leaf cutouts. Have each student tape his hearts to separate green pipe cleaners. Next, stuff pink and red tissue paper into a plastic flowerpot. Then tuck the completed leaves into the pot. This plant is a great decoration for a Valentine's Day party!

Keely Hallin
Bonney Lake Early Childhood Education Assistance Program
Bonney Lake, WA

Chocolate Races

Developing gross-motor skills

Remove the lid from an empty heart-shaped candy box. Place the lid on one side of your classroom and fill it with brown pom-poms (chocolates). Place the bottom of the box across the room. Next, gather a small group of youngsters and have them stand in a line by the lid. The child at the front of the line scoops a chocolate onto a spoon, carefully walks across the room, and deposits the chocolate in the box bottom. He gives the spoon to the next child in line and then goes to the back of the line. Little ones continue until all the chocolates have been transferred to the box bottom.

Angela Norris
West Seneca Christian School
West Seneca, NY

Lollipop Lengths

Measurement: comparing length

To prepare for this partner activity, get a supply of Valentine's Day lollipops. Provide a variety of classroom objects, such as a ruler, scissors, a crayon, a strip of paper, a building block, and a plastic snake. Gather two children and give each one a lollipop. Have a child choose an object and compare it to the length of his lollipop. Then encourage him to say whether the object is longer or shorter than the lollipop. Have his partner repeat the process with a different object. Continue until all the objects have been compared to the lollipops. At the end of the day, have little ones take their special treats home.

Doily Decisions

Expressing oneself through art, writing

These paintings can be left as is, or they can be folded in half to create gorgeous Valentine's Day cards! Gather doilies, paint, paintbrushes, scrap paper, and white construction paper. A child chooses a doily. Then he chooses one of the options below to complete his piece of art.

Option 1: Paint the doily. Then flip it so it's paint-side down on the construction paper. Place scrap paper over the doily and press down to transfer the paint to the paper. Then remove the paper and doily to reveal the print. Repeat the process several times.

Option 2: Place the doily on the construction paper. Paint the doily, making sure the paint is seeping through its holes. Then remove the doily. Repeat the process several times, if desired.

Noel Kuhn
Vermont Hills Family Life Center
Portland, OR

Lovebug Boogie

Letter-sound association

Cut out a copy of the cards on page 286 and place them in a gift bag. Have a child draw a card and name the picture. If the picture name begins with *L*, prompt students to say, "*L* is for *love!*" and then blow a kiss. If the picture name begins with *H*, lead them in saying, "*H* is for *hug!*" and then have them give themselves a hug. If the child draws a picture of a love bug, encourage students to stand up and do their best lovebug boogie!

Picture Cards

Use with "Lovebug Boogie" on page 285.

©The Mailbox®

©The Mailbox®

©The Mailbox®

©The Mailbox®

©The Mailbox®

©The Mailbox®

©The Mailbox®

©The Mailbox®

©The Mailbox®

©The Mailbox®

©The Mailbox®

©The Mailbox®

Exploring Day and Night!

Little ones explore daytime and nighttime with a fun selection of activities that support important preschool skills!

Ten in a Bed

Dramatizing a song, counting backward from ten

Your little ones will love acting out a favorite song about an overcrowded bed! Begin by teaching your youngsters the traditional song "Ten in a Bed." Then place a sheet on the floor so it represents a bed. Have ten students volunteer to lay down on the bed. Then sing the song as your little actors perform the movements, rolling out of the bed when indicated. Repeat the activity until all youngsters have had a turn.

Bright and Shiny Words!

Segmenting words, gross-motor skills

Write the words shown on a sheet of chart paper. Then read them aloud as you follow each word with your finger. Next, read the words again, prompting students to make a circle with their arms to resemble a sun each time you read the word *sun* and pat their legs once when you read the remainder of the word. If desired, repeat a read-aloud of the words the next school day and then have students circle the *sun* in each word with a yellow marker!

Suggested words: *sunlight, sunrise, sunset, sunup, sundown, suntan, sunflower, sunfish, sunbeam, sunburn, sunspot, sunscreen, sundial*

Janet Boyce
Hinojosa Early Childhood and Pre-Kindergarten Center
Houston, TX

Twinkle, Twinkle!

Print awareness: words are separated by spaces

Write the words to "Twinkle, Twinkle, Little Star" on sentence strips and place them in your pocket chart. Die-cut (or punch) several small stars. Gather a small group of students and lead them in singing the song as you follow the words with your finger. Then explain to students that words are groups of letters. There are spaces between words. Next, have a child pick up a star and place it in the space between two words. Continue until each space is covered with a star.

Michael Brink
Westmont Hilltop
Preschool
Johnstown, PA

If desired, repeat this activity, having students place the stars over specific letters!

Which Sticky?

Sorting activities by time of day

Help each child place a white sticky dot (moon) and yellow sticky dot (sun) on separate index fingers. Then name a daily routine (see the suggestions below). Have each child raise her sun in the air if this is something you do in the daytime or the moon if this is something you do at nighttime. (Hint: answers may vary for some suggestions. Some may even require students to raise both fingers!)

Randi Austin
Lebanon, MO

Amy Fishwild
Little Shepherd
    Christian Preschool
Maquoketa, IA

Suggested routines: eat breakfast, go to school, eat lunch, take a bath, listen to a bedtime story, brush your teeth, comb your hair, put on your pajamas, sleep, play on the computer, watch television, wake up, wash your hair, eat dinner

Awake or Asleep?

Sorting, counting, comparing sets

Gather a supply of extra large wiggle eyes and place them in a cup. Have a child gently shake the cup and then spill the eyes. Help students count how many eyes are "awake" (faceup) and how many eyes are "asleep" (facedown). Then have them decide whether there are more eyes awake or asleep. Repeat the activity several times. For an extension, have students write the numbers and the total number of eyes on the board.

Carole L. Watkins, Crown Point, IN

Don't make a peep.
<u>Todd</u> is asleep.

The sun is up today.
It's <u>Todd's</u> time to play.

Don't Make a Peep
Contributing to a class book
For each child, program opposite sides of a sheet of construction paper with the words shown, leaving blanks for the child's name. Take a photo of each child with a blanket over him, holding a teddy bear, and pretending to be asleep. Then take a photo of him standing and looking energetic. Have him glue each photo to the appropriate side of the paper (or have him draw pictures of himself sleeping and awake). Then have him write his name in the space on each side and add sun and moon drawings. Bind the pages together with a cover labeled "Asleep and Awake." Then read the book aloud to your students.

Strange Nighttime Happenings!
Distinguishing real from pretend
What really happens during the night? Youngsters discuss real nighttime happenings and pretend ones with a reading of the almost-wordless book *Tuesday* by David Wiesner. In this story, frogs take flight on a Tuesday night, hovering about on their lily pads. After the read-aloud, have students sing the song shown. Then ask, "What really does happen at nighttime?" Have a student name something realistic that happens at nighttime, such as frogs croaking or people sleeping. Then have a child suggest another animal that wouldn't fly around at night. Repeat the song, inserting the name of the animal, and once again, have a child name a realistic nighttime occurrence. Continue for several rounds.

(sung to the tune of "If You're Happy and You Know It")

When it's nighttime, do the [frogs] all fly around?
When it's nighttime, do the [frogs] all fly around?
That's just silly! [Frogs] don't fly!
You won't see them in the sky.
When it's nighttime, do the [frogs] all fly around?

TUESDAY

DAVID WIESNER

Wonderful WATER

Drip, drop, splish, splash! Little ones explore water with this selection of activities that build important skills.

ideas contributed by Cindy Hoying
Centerville, OH

The Rain Game
Counting, making sets
In advance, place small objects in a lidded container and secure the lid in place. (This will be used as a thunder noisemaker.) Provide a gray cloud cutout, blue pom-poms (raindrops), and a die. Gather a small group of students. Have youngsters take turns rolling the die and placing raindrops on the cloud. When the cloud is full of raindrops, have a child shake the container to represent thunder and then make it rain by picking up the cloud and dropping the raindrops!

Fill 'er Up!
Exploring water and volume
Mark one-inch increments on small clear plastic containers and place them in your water table along with eyedroppers, tablespoons, and straws. Teach youngsters how to place a straw in water, place a finger over the top of the straw, and then raise the straw and deposit the water in a different location. Then encourage youngsters to visit the center and use the instruments to fill up the containers.

 See page 292 for a fine-motor activity.

Spray the Letter
Recognizing letters

Make a splash with this enjoyable literacy activity! Laminate blue raindrop cutouts and use a permanent marker to label each cutout with a different letter. Place the cutouts in an empty sensory table (or on the ground outside). Then give a child a spray bottle filled with water. Name a letter and encourage the child to locate the letter, with help as needed, and spray it. Continue with each letter.

Ripples!
Fine-motor skills, process art

Provide a container of water, an eyedropper, bottle caps in different sizes, a shallow container of blue paint, and construction paper. Gather a small group of students. Then use the eyedropper to make drips on the surface of the water, prompting youngsters to notice the ripples. Give students an opportunity to make drips as well. Then give each child a sheet of construction paper. Have her begin by pressing the largest cap into the paint and then onto her paper several times. Have her repeat the process with each remaining cap, from largest to smallest, making concentric circles. Her art will resemble the ripples on the water's surface.

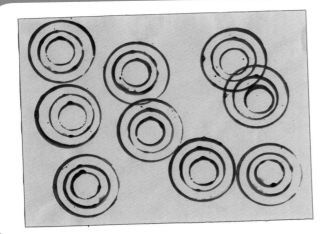

Five Puddles
Developing subtraction skills, exploring evaporation

This simple song and game supports math and science skills. Place five puddle cutouts on the floor and a sun cutout nearby. Lead students in singing the song, prompting volunteers to hold up the sun and remove a puddle when indicated. Have youngsters confirm that there are four puddles on the ground. Then sing the song four more times, reducing the numbers by one each time, until no puddles are left.

(sung to the tune of "Hickory, Dickory, Dock")

Raindrops are falling on down.
[Five] puddles on the ground.
I see the sun.
It dries up one.
Now there are [four] on the ground.

Drip, Drop

Tear.

Glue.

©The Mailbox®

Note to the teacher: Have students tear blue paper to create raindrops.

Drip, Drip, Drop

Making a Glyph

What is a glyph? A glyph is a picture that gives the viewer information. Have your little ones make this rain-themed glyph that is process-art based. Now that's perfect for preschool!

To prepare for this glyph activity, place the materials at your art table. Then follow the steps to help youngsters construct their glyphs. Finally, display the glyphs along with a key and cutout copies of the raindrop characters on page 295. This display is sure to make a splash!

Materials:
cutout copies of the cloud on page 294
9" x 12" light blue construction paper
gray and black crayons
glue
eyedropper
unused toothbrush
blue pom-poms
blue tissue paper squares
slightly diluted dark blue paint

Steps:
1. Give each child a cloud. Have her color her cloud gray. If the child likes rain, have her use the black crayon to draw a happy face on the cloud. If she doesn't, have her draw a frowning face on the cloud. Then have her glue her cloud to the construction paper.
2. If the child is a girl, have her use the eyedropper to drip splotches of blue paint beneath the cloud. If the child is a boy, have him load the toothbrush with paint and then tap it against a finger to spatter little drips of paint below the cloud.
3. Have the child say her age. If she is three years old, have her glue crumpled tissue paper squares below the cloud. If she is four, have her glue pom-poms beneath the cloud.

Cloud Pattern

Use with the glyph activity on page 293.

©The Mailbox®

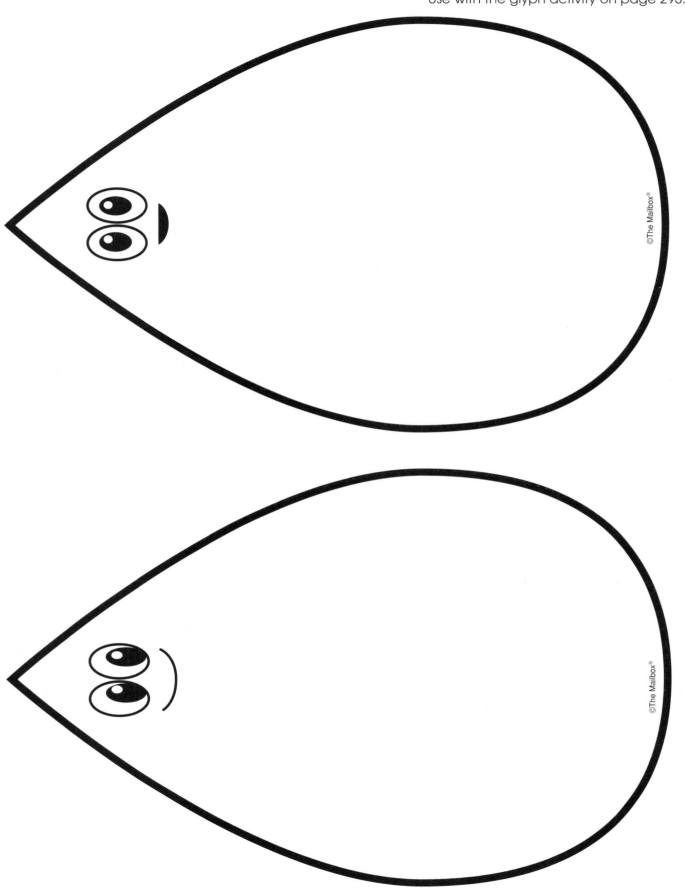

©The Mailbox®

©The Mailbox®

Bunnies Are the Best!

Your little ones will be all ears for activities on those favorite springtime critters—bunnies!

It's a Lineup!

Creating a pattern, one-to-one correspondence

With this math idea, youngsters can make patterns with either bunny noses or bunny tails! In advance, cut out a supply of front-facing and rear-facing bunny patterns (see page 299). Place the cutouts at a center along with colorful pom-poms. Encourage a youngster to visit the center and line up the bunnies. He might choose to line up all front-facing bunnies, to line up all rear-facing bunnies, or to make a pattern with the bunnies. Then the child places pom-pom tails or noses on the bunnies to make a pattern. Pink, blue, pink, blue…

Rosann Eschrich, Phoenix, AZ

Bunny Nests

Investigating living things

Share with students that many bunnies have their babies in shallow nests called *forms*. They line the forms with leaves, grass, and fur. Have little ones make their own bunny forms with this collage project. Provide green or brown paper plates along with leaf cutouts, green paper shreds (grass), and pieces of fake fur. Then make several copies of the front-facing bunny on page 299, reduced in size so they resemble baby bunnies. A child glues leaves, grass, and fur to the form. Then she colors and cuts out baby bunny patterns and glues the cutouts to the form.

Rosann Eschrich

Honey Bunny

Word play, rhyming

This silly game helps little ones develop phonological awareness skills! Get a stuffed rabbit toy (or use a cutout of the front-facing bunny pattern on page 299). Have students sit in a circle. Then hop around the outside of the circle and stop behind a youngster. Say, "Honey, bunny!" and then drop the bunny in the child's lap. When that child stands, sit in her spot. Then prompt her to hop around the circle and repeat the process, naming another word that rhymes with *bunny*. Nonsense words are perfectly acceptable! Continue in the same way.

Sunny bunny!

Bow Tie Bunnies

Adding sets, recognizing numbers

Your youngsters will get these rabbits all dressed up! Make several copies of the bunny and bow tie patterns on page 300. Label each of the bunny ears with dot sets. Then label bow ties with the corresponding sums. Place the bunnies and bow ties at a center. A child counts the dots on both ears, finds the matching bow tie, and places it beneath the bunny.

Toni Foster, Evergreen Avenue Elementary, Woodbury, NJ

Oh So Soft

Writing

Bunny fur is very soft—and so are the projects in this nifty writing activity! Use the front-facing bunny pattern on page 299 to make a construction paper bunny cutout for each child. Have each youngster spread glue on her bunny and then press cotton batting (or cotton balls) over the glue. Next, as each child pets her bunny, have her share the name of another object or animal that feels soft. Write each child's response on a sentence strip. Then display the bunnies and strips in the classroom.

My sweater is soft like this bunny.

Let's Hop
Segmenting words

What do a song, syllables in words, and hopping have in common? Check out this activity! Sing the first verse of the song shown. Have students respond by hopping to your circle time area as they sing the second verse. Next, name a word that is related to Easter, such as one of the suggestions shown. Help students say the word, hopping for each syllable. Repeat with the remaining words.

(sung to the tune of "Short'nin' Bread")

Who can bunny hop,
Hop, hop, hop, hop?
Who can bunny hop
With me now?

We can bunny hop,
Hop, hop, hop, hop.
We can bunny hop
With you now!

Word suggestions:

bunny	egg	Easter
hop	candy	ears
rabbit	basket	flowers
grass	nose	whiskers

So Many Carrots!
Developing fine-motor skills

Have little ones draw a rabbit in the middle of a sheet of paper. Then encourage her to dip the edge of a cosmetic sponge in a shallow container of orange paint and press it on the paper to make prints that resemble carrots. Finally, have her dip her finger in green paint and paint greens on each carrot.

Here's a Little Bunny
Participating in a chant

Here's a little bunny—hop, hop, hop!   *Hold up two fingers and bounce them.*
Here are its long ears—flip, flip, flop!   *Make ears with index fingers.*
It stands very still and wiggles its nose.   *Stand still and wiggle nose.*
Then—zigzag, zigzag—off it goes!   *Place palms together and move them in a zigzag.*

Suzanne Moore, Tucson, AZ

Front-Facing Bunny Pattern
Use with "Where Are the Eggs?" on page 111 , "It's a Lineup!" and "Bunny Nests" on page 296, and "Honey Bunny" and "Oh So Soft" on page 297.

Rear-Facing Bunny Pattern
Use with "It's a Lineup!" on page 296.

Bunny Head and Bow Tie Patterns
Use with "Bow Tie Bunnies" on page 297.

©The Mailbox®

©The Mailbox®

Buzz, Buzz, Buzz!

Little ones build skills with these buzz-worthy activities on bees!

Where Is Bee?

Positional words, speaking in a full sentence

Color and cut out the flower mat on page 304 and cards on page 305. Color and cut out a copy of the bee pattern on page 306. Place the cards facedown near the flower. Then have a child flip a card and use a full sentence to describe the location of the bee. Have a second child place the bee in the identical location in relationship to the flower mat. Continue until all the cards have been flipped over.

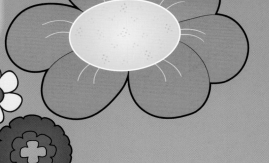

Beginning With *B*.

Make a Print

Beginning sounds

Make a class supply of page 307. Also get a shallow pan of yellow paint and fine-tip black markers. Gather a small group of youngsters and give each child a copy of the page. Have a child name one of the pictures. Prompt little ones to decide if the word begins with /b/ like *bee*. If it does, have the child make a yellow fingerprint on the picture. Continue with each remaining picture. When the paint is dry, have her use a marker to make bee details on each print.

tip → For a less-mess option, simply have little ones stamp the picture with a bee rubber stamp!

Big Bee!

Developing fine-motor skills

This simple craft looks adorable displayed in the classroom with the title "Preschool Is the Place to 'Bee'!" Have each child paint a paper plate yellow (or simply use a yellow plate). Have her attach strips of black electrical tape to the plate to make stripes. Help her trim off any excess tape. Then direct her to attach eye cutouts and a stinger cutout. Finally, prompt her to attach coffee filter wings to the back of the bee. Cute!

Kaila Weingarten
NSCIC Early Head Start
Spring Valley, NY

Hi, Honey!

Following directions

This tasty little snack is easy to whip up! Show students a container of honey and explain that bees use the nectar from flowers to make honey, which is a sweet food. Give each child a small cup with a spoonful of whipped cream cheese. Have him squirt a little honey onto the cream cheese and then mix them together. The child dips pretzel sticks into the mixture or spreads the mixture on crackers or toast. Yum!

Deborah J. Ryan, Newberg, OR

Fuzzy, Buzzy Bee

Recognizing colors

Gather pom-poms of various colors, including several yellow ones, and place them in a container. Have youngsters sit in a circle; then place a yellow beehive cutout (see page 308) in the middle of the circle. Walk around the circle with the container and prompt a child to reach in and pull out a pom-pom. Then have her identify the color. If the pom-pom is yellow (a bee), encourage youngsters to sing the song shown. Then have the child buzz as he "flies" the bee to the hive and then returns to his seat. Continue until each child has had a turn.

(sung to the tune of "London Bridge")

Fuzzy, buzzy bumblebee,
Bumblebee, bumblebee.
Please don't get so close to me!
Bye-bye, bumblebee!

Cindy Hoying
Centerville, OH

From Five to Zero

Subtraction

This action song will be a big hit with your youngsters! Lead students in singing the song five times, reducing the numbers by one each time. During the final verse, change the final line to "Now there are no bees in the air."

(sung to the tune of "Five Green and Speckled Frogs")

[Five] bees fly in the air,
Buzzing from here to there,
Moving as busy as a bee. Ooooh-wee!
One bee then took a dive.
It flew into the hive.
Now there are [four] bees in the air. Beware!

Cindy Hoying
Centerville, OH

"Bee-utiful" Work!

Developing self-esteem

Recognize a job well done with a bee puppet! Transform a bee cutout (see page 306) into a stick puppet. When you see a youngster playing nicely and doing her best, tap the child with the puppet and say, " 'Bee-utiful' work!"

Cindy Hoying

"Bee-utiful" work!

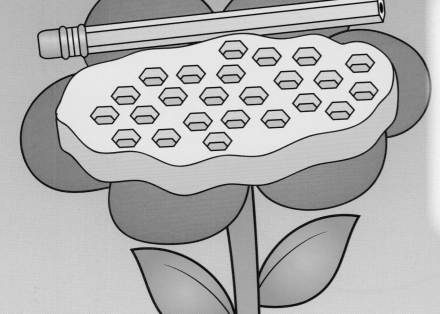

Honeycomb Investigations

Exploring living things, fine-motor skills

Show students a honeycomb (or a picture of a honeycomb). Then explain that the holes in the honeycomb are used by bees to store honey and eggs. Next, give little ones a piece of clay and a pencil. Ask them how they could use the tool (pencil) to make the clay look like a honeycomb. Then have students experiment with the items.

Sarah Friel
St. Paul Day Care
Villa Park, IL

Flower Pattern

Use with "Where Is Bee?" on page 301.

©The Mailbox®

©The Mailbox®

©The Mailbox®

©The Mailbox®

©The Mailbox®

©The Mailbox®

©The Mailbox®

Bee Patterns

Use with "Where Is Bee?" on page 301
and "'Bee-utiful' Work!" on page 303.

©The Mailbox®

©The Mailbox®

Beginning With *B*.

Hive Pattern
Use with "Fuzzy, Buzzy Bee" on page 302.

©The Mailbox®

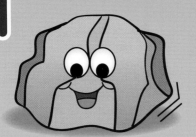

Sand, Soil, and Rocks

With this collection of activities, little ones learn about natural substances and build important skills!

Ideas contributed by Cindy Hoying, Centerville, OH

Teeny Tiny Rocks

Using observation skills, participating in a song

Have students study beach sand with a magnifying glass, leading them to conclude that sand is actually teeny tiny rocks and bits of shell. Waves smash into rocks and shells and, over long periods of time, cause them to break into smaller and smaller pieces, thus making sand. To help youngsters remember the information, lead them in singing the action song shown.

(sung to the tune of "If You're Happy and You Know It")

Oh, my sand is made of rocks and bits of shell,	*Cup hands.*
And the waves have crashed and smashed it up so well	*Clap hands together.*
That it feels so very neat	*Do the twist.*
On the beach beneath my feet.	
Oh, my sand is made of rocks and bits of shell.	*Cup hands.*

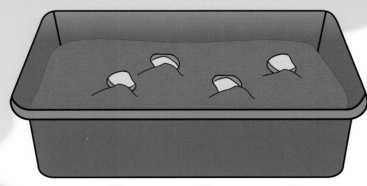

Rocks in the Soil

Ordering numbers

Gather several medium-size smooth rocks. (You can use found rocks or ones purchased at a craft store.) Use a white, silver, or black permanent marker to write a different number from 1 to 10 on each rock. Place the rocks in a tub of soil and provide a chubby paintbrush. A child finds a rock and brushes off the soil. Then she sets aside the rock. When she finds all the rocks in the tub, she places them in numerical order and counts the rocks aloud. (If desired, provide a number line for reference.)

Looking for a Rock
Identifying rhyming words

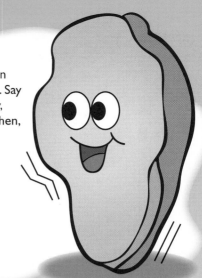

Rhyming words rock! Lead students in singing the first verse of the song. When you're finished, tell students that you notice there are rhyming words in the song. Say the third line, pausing to have children provide the final word in the line. Then say, "Yes, *go* and *slow* rhyme!" Continue with each remaining verse in the same way. Then, if possible, take students outside for a rock search!

(sung to the tune of "The Farmer in the Dell")

I'm looking for a rock.
I'm looking for a rock.
I'll go so nice and slow,
Just looking for a rock.

Continue with the following: *I'll jog around a bog, I'll look beside a brook, I'll hike to where I like*

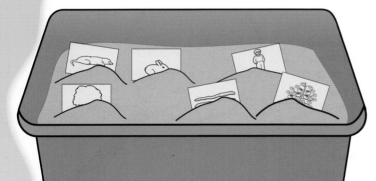

Who Needs Soil?
Investigating living things

Make a copy of the cards on page 311 and place them facedown. Place soil in a tub. To begin, have a child flip a card and identify the picture. Prompt little ones to discuss why the item pictured needs soil, leading them to the conclusion listed below. Then have the child place the card in the tub of soil. Continue with each remaining card.

rabbit: digs a burrow in the soil, eats plants grown in soil
tree: roots go into the soil to bring the tree nourishment
person: eats fruit and vegetables that are grown in soil
earthworm: lives in the soil
mole: lives in the soil
tomato plant: roots go into the soil to bring the plant nourishment

All About My Rock
Recording observations

Have each child bring a rock to school. Gather two or three children with their rocks and give each child a copy of page 312. Have her draw her rock. Then, help her answer the questions about it. Afterward, label each rock with the appropriate student's name and place it at your science center along with magnifying glasses. Then little ones can explore and compare the rocks!

©The Mailbox®

©The Mailbox®

©The Mailbox®

©The Mailbox®

©The Mailbox®

©The Mailbox®

My Rock

 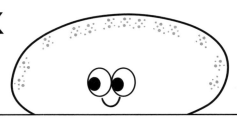

🖍 **This is my rock.**

My rock is small **medium** **large**.

My rock is **smooth** **rough**.

My rock is **shiny** **dull**.

©The Mailbox®

INDEX